MW01286777

A BUSINESS CARD

How to Turn Your Book into 18 Streams of Income

KARY OBERBRUNNER

Wall Street Journal and *USA Today* Bestselling Author

Senior Editor: Erin Casey
Developmental Edit: Tina Morlock
Project Manager: Crissy Maier
Cover Design: Debbie O'Byrne

ethos
collective

Printed in the United States of America

Published by Ethos Collective™
PO Box 43, Powell, OH 43065
EthosCollective.vip

LCCN: 2021915903
Paperback ISBN: 978-1-63680-059-2
Hardback ISBN: 978-1-63680-064-6
e-book ISBN: 978-1-63680-060-8

Available in paperback, e-book, and audiobook

Some names and identifying details have been changed to protect the
privacy of individuals.

For our Author Academy Elite and Ethos Clients
You are the story.

A special thank you to the Igniting Souls Publishing Agency
Global Team
I couldn't have done this book without you.

For Special Bonus Content Associated with This Book,
Including the 19th Stream of Income, Visit:

KaryOberbrunner.com/18Book

CONTENTS

NOTE TO THE READER

WHY ALL THE QR CODES?

I'm a visual learner. Tell me and I may listen. Show me and I will understand. For this reason, throughout the book, I'm going to include QR codes that you can scan if you're interested in seeing what I mean via demonstration and illustration.

I'm passionate about helping authors extract every ounce of potential from their book and book-based business. For this reason, in addition to *telling you* with my words, I'm also *showing you* with my work.

If visual learning isn't your thing or if you find QR codes distracting, then just skip that part. But if you want to learn from my countless author mistakes, then simply scan the QR codes (like the one below) with your smart phone camera or click the links if you're reading this in an e-book format. My belief is that all of my research and development (a.k.a. failure) could save you hundreds of hours and thousands of dollars.

I don't mind being a trailblazer. It helps me learn what works and what doesn't work.

The rest of this book is the 18 Streams of Income Model© that has helped me and many of the 250,000+ authors I've trained during the past twenty years.

It's about to get exciting. Enjoy the journey.

Bonus Content

INTRODUCTION: ONCE UPON A TIME

Once upon a time, I was a poor author. Oh, sure, I could write well enough, and I was good at crafting a compelling message. Ability wasn't the issue. Money was. Maybe we share a similar story. (Or maybe parts of a similar story.)

For as long as I remember, I wanted to write a book that changed people's lives, or more specifically, ignited their souls. I didn't want to get rich or become famous. I just wanted to earn enough money to leave my day job and live my passion of writing books and igniting souls full time.

A small, traditional house published my first book in 2004, back when I had hair—or at least a little of it. Then, I waited. I imagined the royalties rolling in. The thought of handing in my two-week notice hijacked my brain often. After all, I had a traditional publishing deal, and my book would be in brick-and-mortar stores.

Then again, my big advance from my publishing deal was *zero*—as in nothing. I was a first-time author, and my unproven track record made the small publisher nervous. It made me nervous, too, especially when I opened my first royalty check. It was so large, my wife, Kelly, and I celebrated with dinner at a moderately priced restaurant.

We didn't have any kids at the time, which meant our expenses were lower than they are now. Even so, after doing the math, I figured I would need at least fifty more royalty checks to replace my normal income—for a month.

It was pretty bad.

Then, I had a brilliant idea. I would write a second book. That way the income would roll in twice as fast.

Nope, it still wasn't enough.

So I decided I would write a few more books. Books three and four came out with the help of a traditional publisher. This time, I received $36,000 for that two-book deal, spread out over three years. If you're doing the math, you already know that, while better than zero, that advance wasn't enough to live on.

Then came baby one, baby two, and baby three. The advances from the third book paid for some mighty fine diapers, formula, baby wipes, cribs, and strollers.

Who was I fooling?

I'd never earn enough by writing books to replace my income. Self-doubt and dashed dreams stole my sleep and patience—oftentimes in the same night. Those babies needed time, and I couldn't justify working all day at my real job, then spending much of the night writing the next book half asleep in the recliner. Morning after morning, I'd wake up completely drained and flabbergasted at (not to mention disappointed by) the new paragraphs that appeared in my manuscript. I honestly couldn't even remember typing those words the night before.

But then, something different happened with book four: *Your Secret Name* (YourSecretName.com). Instead of putting a book into the world and hoping for the best, I turned that book into additional streams of income.

It started with a one-day workshop for my church and community. To my surprise, a few dozen people showed up and even paid a small fee to attend. Then someone asked to get certified to use the content from the book in her life-coaching practice. She even offered to pay. Other people requested materials to teach the book to their friends and families, which led me to create a five-session course complete with a short guidebook.

Inspired by the momentum of success, my creativity kicked into high gear. I ended up developing even more income streams using the book's content—eighteen in all. My dream was finally building steam, and my book was earning me a small but decent side income. Over time, that side income grew my bank account and my confidence.

I took the same approach with book five, *The Deeper Path* (DeeperPathBook.com), a personal growth book. Using those same eighteen streams of income brought even more success, because this time I knew my strategy before publishing the book. Finally, I could see a light at the end of the day-job tunnel.

Having proved to myself it could be possible to earn enough as an author to replace my income, I felt (sort of) confident enough to take a big risk and quit my day job. Honestly, I was scared to death to become a full-time entrepreneur. Remember, we had three kids under the age of six. But Kelly gave me the okay (and the encouragement) to take the leap—as long as I promised to bring in the money. She worked part time as a counselor, but her ten hours a week wouldn't replace my income.

Call it naivete or faith—I had more than enough of both —but I vowed to myself to succeed. In my mind, there was no other option or plan B. I created eighteen streams of income for book six, a business book called *Day Job to Dream Job* (DayJobToDreamJob.com). I experimented with the different streams of income and switched out a couple. Once again, the model produced the same result, a six-figure business—that's a six-figure business for *each* book to which I applied my 18 Streams of Income Model©.

By this time, several of the clients I had gained through my book-based live coaching programs started asking for my secret sauce. They wanted to write books and turn them into eighteen streams of income too. I was too inexperienced to take their questions seriously, so I brushed them off, thinking they were only humoring me.

After several people came back with even more conviction and more questions, I finally got the hint. In 2014, I launched my own publishing company, Author Academy Elite (AuthorAcademyElite.com), with the goal of teaching people how to become profitable authors. I committed to helping them turn their books into eighteen streams of income so they could do what they love full time. But that was only part of my reason for launching Author Academy Elite. I still wanted to change lives and ignite souls. My thought was that by teaming up with other like-minded authors, *together*, we could ignite even more souls by publishing incredible books.

In 2016, I tried using the same model with a fiction book. I had never written a fiction book, and many skeptics told me the model wouldn't work. They taunted me on webinars, blog posts, and emails, saying, "You can't turn a fiction book into eighteen streams of income."

Nothing fires me up more than people's unbelief. I took it as a challenge and wrote *Elixir Project*, a dystopian young adult thriller about people's minds getting hacked. I launched the book at a global livestream party. Soon afterward I launched a subsequent course, conference, and a mastermind coaching program—all based on a fiction book.

By this time, I had gathered a team to help me, and together we generated six figures in six weeks with *Elixir Project*.

In the past seventeen years, I've trained more than 250,000 authors from all over the world on this model. It works across cultures, languages, and genres. From our best estimates, we believe these authors have impacted another 26 million people with the books they've published.

Although I've done countless interviews and webinars on this topic, to date, I've never published the 18 Streams of Income Model in a real book. *Entrepreneur* Magazine ran a feature article on our model in which it highlighted many case studies from our actual clients. View that article here (Entrepreneur.com/article/358499) or scan the QR code.

Entrepreneur Article

Based on the many nudges from clients and team members, I finally agreed, this past summer, to write such a book. I put aside the other book I was working on, and *Your Book is NOT a Business Card* poured out of me in a matter of weeks. It's my deep honor to guide you in this exciting journey. I hope it enriches you, your readers, and your clients the same way it has me and mine.

So are you ready to write a new story for yourself as an author?

If so, let's begin by busting a few myths that might be impeding your success.

1

BOOKS AND BUSINESS CARDS ARE DIFFERENT

Before we get into the specifics of the 18 Streams of Income Model, I need to dispel a few myths about books and publishing, and the fallacies that keep most authors poor. We hear so much about starving artists (which include authors), and the assumption is that most creative people spend all their lives hovering around the poverty line.

But it doesn't have to be that way.

As with most things in life, you have to have the right mindset about your book and your opportunities as an author if you want to shift from poor to profitable.

So let's start with the big one—the myth that can kill your chance for success as an author faster than any other.

What is that myth?

Namely, that your book is your business card.

Have you heard it? I have, and it's bad advice taught as truth by experts all over the world. It's heralded by many influencers as a smart and savvy belief.

But the authors who internalize this myth pay dearly.

If this is a belief that you have accepted as true, or maybe even have shared, don't despair. Throughout our journey, we'll unpack why this belief is lethal to your success as an author. Better yet, I'll provide you with an alternative mindset that will set you up for success.

If you're ready, let's bust this myth with logic as we look at the differences between business cards and books:

Business cards cost money. **Books create value.**

Business cards don't create value. When someone hands us a tiny piece of cardstock with their name and contact info on it, we might glance at it and say thank you. But before long, that business card ends up in the trash bin. *If* we keep the card, it goes into a pile with all the other business cards we never look at.

Business cards hold no inherent value. You can't resell them or find a website that offers used ones. If you visit the library, the librarian won't help you find business cards on the shelf.

Think about universities. Even though their shelves are already well-stocked with books, professors are often warned to *publish or perish.* They aren't told to print a business card or perish. Why is this? It's because books create value and establish credibility for the professor as well as for the university. Published authors and their books bring additional notoriety to the institution. Printing more worthless business cards? Not so much.

Business cards are an expense. **Books are an asset.**

Business cards are a business expense. Books are investments that turn into assets.

No one brings people onstage with an introduction that includes the byline of "the creator of such-and-such business card." Speakers all around the world, however, step onto stages right after hearing the words, "Please welcome the author of such-and-such book."

We don't give awards to the best business card, nor do we have business card agents who shop around for stellar business card proposals.

Most people don't put business cards on their Christmas wish list. We don't wrap them up as gifts. Parents don't read business cards to their children at bedtime. Oprah hasn't launched a business card club or made anyone famous because of their business card design.

We don't put a dust jacket on a business card to protect it. Nor are business cards given as reading assignment in schools.

People don't wait in line for a celebrity to autograph their business card. No one makes the rounds on television shows to talk about the business card they made. Business card creators don't line up multi-city tours to talk about their latest designs.

Authors seek out forewords and endorsements for their books and even create book trailers. But no one asks for someone to do the same for his or her business card. Creating a trailer for your business card would be a waste of time and money.

According to a survey cited in *The New York Times*, 81 percent of the population dreams of writing a book, but they don't feel the same way about creating a business card.[1] Companies don't offer movie deals based on business cards. Foreign countries aren't lining up to translate business cards. We don't invest resources to create updated and expanded versions of business cards.

My guess is you're starting to see how ridiculous it is to compare a book to a business card. And yet, in many circles, people accept this destructive myth as truth.

Business cards decrease pocket space. **Books increase your influence, impact, and income.**

I'll keep the illustration comparing books and business cards going just a little bit longer.

If you dream of people buying your business card at night while you sleep, then you're going to be disappointed. Passive income is a real possibility for books, but not for business cards.

Carpenters might specialize in making bookshelves but not business card shelves. We don't hire ghostwriters and developmental editors to create our business cards. Such a practice would be a waste of money because it wouldn't yield a return on investment.

A business card *points you in the right direction* to a business that can solve your problem, whereas a book *is the right direction*. It's a solution to your problem. Some might say that distinction is simply semantics, splitting hairs. But this couldn't be further from the truth. It's on par with saying that an automobile magazine is the same thing as an automobile. You won't get anywhere if you try to ride your magazine to the grocery store. An automobile magazine tells you about the vehicle. It may contain pictures of the vehicle, but its purpose is to inform. The purpose of the vehicle is to transport you to another destination.

Similarly, the purpose of a business card is to inform. The purpose of a book is to transport you to another world or empower you to transform your life.

Business cards get thrown away. **Books last forever.**

Unlike business cards, books contain strange magical powers. We don't excavate the earth looking for business cards from former generations.

Tyrannical governments never initiated business card burning events. If you Google book burning, however, you'll see plenty of dark moments throughout history when such events took place because people feared the power of books.

My recent internet search revealed some other noteworthy beliefs about books. Evidently, some of the most popular searches related to books are the following:

Is it a sin to throw away a *book*?

Is it illegal to throw away a *book*?

Where can I donate unwanted *books*?

Why did people send soldiers their unwanted *books*?

Now, replace the word *book* with *business card*.

Is it a sin to throw away a *business card*?

Is it illegal to throw away a *business card*?

Where can I donate unwanted *business cards*?

Why did people send soldiers their unwanted *business cards*?

People don't search for answers to questions like those regarding business cards. Throwing away a business card is such a common practice, we don't think twice about doing it.

Books occupy a place of reverence in our minds. This belief has been indelibly engraved in our hearts and minds. Nate Pepper offers the reason for our innate respect for books: "Physical, printed books are synonymous with learning, opportunity, and freedom of speech. To casually discard, or worse, destroy a book is disrespectful and undemocratic."[2]

Books travel throughout the millennia. Business cards, however, die a forgettable death.

Business cards change landfills. **Books change lives.**

No one ever said, "This business card changed my life." They don't utter these words because the only thing a business card changes is the amount of space in a landfill. Many people, however, have described a book as life changing.

People post reviews for books on websites and write articles about them for newspapers and magazines. These reviews explain how the book touched or entertained or inspired them to live in a new, better, stronger, healthier, or more vibrant, authentic way. The same cannot be said for business cards. I've never found a website that reviews business cards. Notice Luisa Plaja's five steps for writing a book review below.[3] Imagine the absurdity of redirecting her advice for writing a business card review.

How to Write a Business Card Review

1. Start with a couple of sentences describing what the *business card* is about.
2. Discuss what you particularly liked about the *business card*.
3. Mention anything you disliked about the *business card*.
4. Round up your review.
5. You can give the *business card* a rating.

Business cards seek to inform. **Books seek to transform.**

I cringe when people refer to books as business cards because the difference between books and business cards is clear. Still, this myth prevails in some circles, and I don't know why. It's an offense to the author, the reader, the book, and the industry. Believing the myth, as I mentioned earlier, kills your chances of building wealth as an author. If you view your book as a business card, you will never be able to position yourself to receive the maximum amount of income from your book.

But even if you couldn't care less about growing your income or credibility, I'm certain you can see the biggest distinction between books and business cards: Business cards seek to inform. Books seek to transform readers' lives.

I know this truth firsthand because several books have changed my life.

For starters, the Bible has shaped the way I see myself, the world, and God. Other books have inspired me to make major shifts in my life—like *The $100 Startup* by Chris Guillebeau.[4] My wife bought it for me at a time when I needed vision. It helped me believe my dream job was possible, and it gave me the courage to take action. I applied the principles from his book and turned my passion into my full-time gig.

Many of my friends and family members asked me how I made the shift from employee to entrepreneur. I captured my process in writing and turned it into my own book, called *Day Job to Dream Job*.

After reading my book, an Australian entrepreneur sent me the following email. Although I've never met Kate Taylor, evidently in her own words, *Day Job to Dream Job* "changed her life."

> There is a man who wrote a book called *Day Job to Dream Job*. I read it because I needed some real ideas on how to get out of working full time in a job I wasn't happy in. It changed my life, and here I am, running my own business. So, thank you, Kary Oberbrunner, for taking the time to put your thoughts down on paper for people like me who just needed some clarity on how to make the jump.

Think about the levels of impact just in this story. I read Chris's book and it changed my life. Then I wrote *Day Job to Dream Job* and it changed Kate's life. Kate in turn will change someone else's life, and the circle of impact continues. This can be true for you too. There's a world in need of your book, and the more streams of income you leverage, the greater your circle of influence and the more impact you'll make.

In the following chapters, you'll learn how I've used this model to create multiple six-figure businesses with books in multiple genres, including fiction. Most recently, my team and I created a seven-figure launch with my book *Unhackable* (UnhackableBook.com).

Money might excite some readers, and to be honest, I enjoy the security and opportunities having money affords. Something else, however, excites me even more: igniting souls. A few years back, I received a handwritten card in the mail. It came from a young woman who had read *Your Secret Name* and joined the related live coaching program. Here's what she said:

> Thank you for your gift of journeying through the *Your Secret Name* program. My roommate has gone the longest she has ever gone without acting out her eating disorder, over three months now.
>
> By going through the program together, so many deep spiritual things were brought up that we had never discussed together. We had some incredible conversations and were challenged with so many things to think about and talk to God about.
>
> I feel it helped me in my intimacy with Jesus. I feel like I grew in the ability to ask God really genuine questions, and I feel like he revealed His love for me in a new way. You are a wise and godly man, and I am so thankful that you are willing not only to share your story but also to provide a safe and beautiful place for others to share theirs. Thank you for your gift! Two lives were changed!

If you haven't received a letter like this yet, hang on a

little longer because you will. I'm deeply honored that you're willing to dive into this book. Your goal might be to earn more influence, impact, or income (Hopefully, all three!). Regardless, it's my privilege to show you the model.

Let's roll!

2

POOR AUTHORS AND SMART AUTHORS ARE DIFFERENT

`The way we think about our books shapes the results we experience.`

Casual observers might think the difference between poor authors and smart authors is all about the words on the page. Of course, content is important. We've all been disappointed to read an overrated book with a ton of sizzle and no substance. And we've been blown away by an underrated book with no sizzle but a ton of substance.

Yes, content matters. But too often, authors overestimate the power of their content and underestimate the personal mindset that drives (or stalls) their success. It's this mindset that positions them and their books well in the marketplace. An author's mindset is a key factor in creating the essential *sizzle* that attracts readers. Although it might sound a little cheesy, it's true. Without the sizzle, books fizzle.

Smart authors leverage both sizzle and substance. In this chapter, you'll see the dichotomy between smart authors and poor authors and why each generates entirely different results.

Poor authors think their book is about them. **Smart authors know their book is about their readers.**

It's your book. You wrote it. You're the one who invested the required blood, sweat, and tears to get it done. Therefore, it's all about you, right?

Only if you want to remain a poor author.

Smart authors recognize their books are all about their audience—their struggles and fears, their angst, and their needs. By stepping into the mind of the reader, the smart author becomes aware of how to deliver the message in a way that serves the audience.

When our eyes are on ourselves, we lose our ability to show up filled up. We focus on our performance rather than our presence. Our readers feel the distance, and we lose connection. No one likes to feel used—especially the people shelling out hard-earned money for the books they read. If you make them feel like they exist to serve your ego or grow your income, you'll break rapport—and they'll move on to someone else who appreciates them.

Poor authors view their book as the end of a relationship. **Smart authors view their book as the start of a relationship.**

If all you have to offer your audience is your book, then once a reader buys your book, the relationship is over.

This is exactly what happened with my first three books. My goal was to get people to buy my book. But then what? I'd autograph the book and wonder what else I should say with my signature. "See you in the afterlife?" I didn't know. I wasn't being morbid, just realistic. I had nothing else to offer.

Once the reader reached The End, our relationship ended.

This mindset was one reason I stayed a poor author for so long. There was no next step, no way to contact me for more information, coaching, or anything else. Even if every reader bought all three of my books, the only way I was ever going to be able to leave my day job that way was to write and sell a *ton* more books.

Then with my fourth book, *Your Secret Name*, everything changed.

I knew the content of the book had the power to change lives. But to really ignite souls, I knew I also needed more ways to interact with my readers. With this new mindset, I wrote my book with the intention of sharing its content from the stage in front of thousands of people. I created opportunities that moved the reader to action as they read the book. Through a journey of online assessments and bonuses revealed within the book, I created an interactive experience. As the reader progressed through the book, our relationship grew. And at the end, I included back ads that directed the reader on what to do next to continue the relationship.

With that book, I took the first few steps in a series of smart steps that moved me from poor to profitable.

Poor authors view their book as a single product. **Smart authors view their book as an integrated product suite.**

In 2021, Apple became the most valuable company in the world.

Although many strategic factors contribute to this ranking, one main reason for its financial success is the company's commitment to creating an integrated product suite. This means your Apple Watch pairs with your MacBook Pro, which works with your iPad, which talks with your iPhone, which transmits to your AirPods, and so on.

In other words, each of Apple's many products function together as one. They constitute an integrated product suite that makes the overall experience more valuable to the user.

Rather than the company needing to acquire more and

more new customers, they simply upsell, cross-sell, and down-sell their existing customers. They even provide a free music service, iTunes, to organize and play your music. This onboards potential customers and entices them to join the Apple family.

Similarly, smart authors recognize that a book is not a stand-alone product. Instead, they publish each book as part of an integrated product suite. Such authors might provide a free chapter, article, or assessment based on the book to familiarize their potential customers with their content. The free content creates rapport and builds the know-like-trust factor between the author and reader.

Once readers enter the author's ethos, it's much easier to keep them moving down the buyer's journey. (We'll unpack the finer points of this exciting journey in the upcoming chapters.)

Poor authors launch their book once. **Smart authors launch their book time and time again.**

Poor authors think it's one and done. They exert a ton of energy launching the book, and when the event is over, so are their marketing efforts. This experience proves draining on author and reader alike.

Often authors experience the "baby blues" after bringing their book into the world. The launch process sometimes creates an adrenaline rush, and authors can feel depressed afterward or experience a dip in energy levels. The sense that "it's all over" magnifies a sense of loss. The launch is done, and there's nothing left to do.

Smart authors engage in micro launches. They launch again and again in different ways. They might create a launch for different versions of their book: softcover, hardcover, e-book, and audiobook.

They might launch their book on different social media

platforms. Or they create separate in-person launches for friends and family, coworkers, alma maters, and previous places of residence.

Your book is always new to the person who's never read it, which means you always have new opportunities with new audiences. I've known many authors who celebrate their book's "birthday" each year. Another strategy is linking your book to a special day. There are plenty of free calendars online that list National Days. Here are a few:

- DaysOfTheYear.com
- NationalToday.com/national-day-calendar
- Calendarr.com

By finding observance days with which your book connects, you can "newsjack" even the most random holidays and build some buzz around your book. "Newsjack" is a term established by David Meerman Scott in 2011, which leverages breaking news to draw eyes to your organization, cause, or book—in the context of our conversation.[15]

As long as you're savvy with newsjacking, most people will perceive you as relevant and helpful. The key is to focus on serving your audience, not selling your book.

Poor authors focus on selling their book. **Smart authors focus on serving their audience.**

Serving others means showing up filled up. Selling others means showing up empty. In my book *Show Up Filled Up*, I explain the difference in detail, but if you look around, you'll quickly notice a short supply of people who genuinely show up filled up. Those who show up filled up are outliers—they aren't the norm. They give with the expectation of growing, helping, and uplifting *others*.

In contrast, there are plenty of people in the world who

are willing to help—as long as they get something in return. These transactional types are average. Even more common are the people who entirely ignore the call to be helpful.

Because of the shortage of people who give and live generously, if you choose to show up filled up, you have an opportunity to stand out. By being valuable, you'll become visible. Make it a lifestyle, and the world will sit up and take notice. When this happens, you become irreplaceable.

So what does showing up filled up and serving your audience look like for an author? It means when you show up for a television, radio, or podcast interview, you provide helpful information to the audience, and in doing so, make the host look good. You serve the listeners and your host. If you have three steps, you give all three steps. You go above and beyond. You mention your free assessment for those who want to go deeper.

Selling the audience feels very different. It means you stop short of sharing all three of your steps in the interview and end with, "You need to buy my book to get the third and final step." The audience feels the difference between a generous author and a stingy one. One author is smart, and the other remains poor.

I know you're reading this book because you don't want to be a poor author. You want to be a smart author—a profitable author who uses words to transform lives and ignite souls. That's what I want for you too. The eighteen streams of income (actually *nineteen* because I've included a bonus) will put you on the path to building a six- or even seven-figure business with your book. But it all starts with your mindset— what you believe about your book and yourself paves the way for your success as an author.

Sizzle *and* substance. Remember. Both are necessary.

Now, let's start putting these powerful streams of income to work for your book.

● 3

INCOME STREAMS 1-4

> People prefer your book in the format
> of their choice.

The more formats you provide, the more readers you'll have, which is why the first four income streams we'll discuss are all about delivery. Before you can leverage the more innovative income streams, you have to take care of essentials. Income streams 5 through 18 build off the book itself, so it behooves you to create and then leverage income streams 1 through 4 first. Failing to do so will exponentially decrease your influence, impact, and income.

Modern technology enables authors to publish books in multiple formats, and there's no reason not to cash in. The additional time and money to release these other versions are nominal and set you up to reach more people and earn more money.

#1: SOFTCOVERS SELL

Softcovers, also known as paperbacks, are inexpensive to produce because of the paperboard cover and glued binding.

Traditional publishers prefer this cheaper version when they want to release a book without taking a risk. Many first editions today are released as paperbacks. If and when a book earns bestseller status, the traditional publisher may create a hardcover version of the book. (See income stream 2.)

Smart authors leverage the softcover version by offering multiple-copy or bulk-buy discounts, especially at book launches and book signings. If your black-and-white paperback retails at $15 each and comes in cases of twenty-four copies, you may want to consider the following multiple-copy discount:

1 Copy = $15 or $15 each
10 Copies = $125 or $12.50 each
24 Copies = $240 or $10 each

#2: HARDCOVERS IMPRESS

I've come to love hardcovers, also referred to as hardback, hardbound, and case-bound. The hard protective cover, typically made of binder's board or heavy paperboard covered with cloth, heavy paper, or even leather, gives the book a classy, more permanent look and feel.

Hardcover books play a different role in the buyer's journey from the paperback. They're meant to impress because they look better and feel better to the touch.

Consequently, they're more expensive to produce. Often hardcovers contain a flexible, sewn spine. This allows the book to lie flat on a surface when opened. Hardcover books' pages are often higher quality than those of softcover books, which contributes to the durability of the book.

Many hardcovers also come with a dust jacket or dust cover. Case laminate covers are another option in which the cover design is printed directly onto the board binding. You can even opt for a case laminate with a dust jacket. (I always encourage authors to leverage the extra space on the dust jacket flaps to tell the reader more about their brand or business.)

Hardcovers are more costly to produce than paperbacks, but they are also more impressive to certain buyers. Smart authors order hardcover books in bulk to reduce their overall cost. They also plan ahead and leverage the extended delivery time option. (Rush-delivery costs can take a bite out of profits.) Planning ahead can reduce the cost of hardcover production down to a couple dollars difference from paperback, thus increasing the profit margin.

I refer to hardcovers as *influencer copies*. Mailing influencers a hardcover copy of your book with a personal note creates quite an impression. Increase the impact by integrating an influencer box. You can view a picture of my influencer box by scanning the QR code below. Notice which version of the book I included in the box—definitely not a softcover.

Influencer Box

#3: E-BOOKS TRAVEL EVERYWHERE

You may not have a book within five feet of you at any given moment. But you're probably within five feet of your phone. The same is true for the bulk of humans—day in and day out.

This is good news for authors because every smartphone is an e-book reader. If you publish a book but don't turn it into an e-book, you are leaving money on the table—a whole bunch of it.

The term *e-book* is short for electronic book. This popular format first became available in the 2000s, and by 2010, it overtook hardcover sales. Low prices, ease of portability, and frictionless purchasing contributed to this rise in sales. Consumers can browse through titles online, select, order, pay for, and have their e-book purchase delivered in a matter of seconds to their computers, phones, tablets, or e-book readers.

Some authors only release their books in the form of an e-book because the cost to produce them is so low and the earning potential is high. Authors can earn up to 70 percent royalties on e-book sales. When compared with what traditionally published authors often receive in royalties for their physical book—15 percent or less—e-book royalties can really add up.

Smart authors leverage their books in the e-book format. Research I uncovered when writing *Unhackable* reveals why.[1] The average person spends a total of five hours a day browsing the web and using apps on their smartphone. This equates to around a third of the time we are awake, and it's twice as much as we think we spend.

Check out these other smartphone statistics below. Realize your e-book could be the content of choice for many of your readers while scrolling their phones.[2]

- 46 percent of Americans admit to checking their smartphones before they even get out of bed in the morning.[3]
- 75 percent of people keep their phones on all day and night, not turning them off to go to bed.[4]
- 84 percent of people say they couldn't even give up their smartphone for a single day.[5]
- 88 percent of Americans admit to using their

smartphones while in the bathroom. (The other 12 percent might be lying.)[6]

- Nearly three in four American smartphone users surveyed said they are within five feet of their devices most of the time.[7]

Although I cited the above statistics in *Unhackable* to show how addictive and distracting smartphones can be, look for the positive application in our conversation. Because your book provides life-changing content, it has the opportunity to influence many more people through the form of an e-book.

#4: AUDIOBOOKS LEVERAGE NONCOGNITIVE ACTIVITIES

David Goggins authored the book *Can't Hurt Me.*[8] I spoke with his publisher, who told me that out of the millions of copies sold at that time, many were in the form of an audiobook.

Guess the percentage. Maybe 5 percent or 10 percent?

Fifty-eight percent of the copies sold…were audiobooks! Goggins is not an anomaly. Audiobooks have been the fastest-growing publishing version of books for multiple years. Here are three reasons why audiobooks are exploding in popularity:

1. Audiobook players (a.k.a. smartphones) are easily accessible.
2. Audiobooks create an entirely different experience than reading (the spoken word adds a new dynamic).
3. Audiobooks allow us to do two things at once (one cognitive and one noncognitive).

Although the "talking book" has been around since the 1930s, recent advances in technology have made this medium the preferred choice for many people. Audiobooks began as records and then moved to many other mediums, including cassette tapes, compact discs, and today digital files. In the 1980s, book retailers started displaying audiobooks on bookshelves.

Audiobook subscription services have helped this medium rise in popularity during the past decade. Audiobook sales in the United States in 2019 totaled $1.2 billion, up 16 percent from the previous year. In addition to the increase in sales, Edison Research's national survey of American audiobook listeners ages eighteen and up found that the average number of audiobooks listened to per year increased to 8.1 in 2020, up from 6.8 in 2019.[912]

About ten years ago, I gave Audible (an audiobook subscription service; bit.ly/FreeAudibleLink) a try. As a business owner, husband, and the father of three kids, I didn't have a ton of extra time to sit down and read books. Over the next sixty days, while running, driving, or mowing the lawn, I listened to a couple of audiobooks. I loved it so much I kept my subscription. For a low monthly fee, to this day, I still choose a new audiobook and listen to it each month. If I blow through those audiobooks, I buy more credits.

I listen to audiobooks because I want to redeem my time. And I am not alone. Business guru Brian Tracy reveals what's possible in our daily drive time. The average person commutes 12,000 to 25,000 miles per year, which works out to between 500 and 1,000 hours per year.[1013] If you prefer public transportation, the illustration still works.

You can become an expert in your field by simply listening to educational audio programs as you ride from place to place. Studies reveal that listening to audio programs while commuting can equate to earning a doctorate-level degree in your topic of focus.

In addition to earning royalties on their audiobook sales, authors can earn even more from Audible for sharing their audiobooks with others. Most authors don't realize that when they put their book on Audible.com, they receive a bounty link to share with friends, family members, clients, and potential readers. When someone uses the bounty link to start a subscription, that person gets a free audiobook. Additionally, the author who shared the link receives a $70 "bounty" for each new subscription over 60 days.

With that said, here are the links to my audiobooks. You can listen to a sample of each one for free. Listen to the intro and outro in my audiobooks, and you'll see how we lead listeners back to free bonuses that integrate them into our buyer's journey. Many of these bonuses leverage email list-building strategies and marketing funnel tactics. Listen and you'll see what I mean.

Show Up Filled Up

Unhackable

The Deeper Path

Your Secret Name

Elixir Project

Day Job to Dream Job

Audiobook royalties add up quickly. If your books aren't on audio, you're missing a huge opportunity. Jump into the audiobook world with a free trial subscription: bit.ly/FreeAudibleLink. Once you listen to a few audiobooks, you'll realize the incredible opportunity for increasing your influence, impact, and income.

Audible

Pro Tip

If you're not keen on reading your own audiobook, don't worry. I wasn't about to narrate my fiction book *Elixir Project*. With all the characters, I would have had to do over two dozen accents. No thank you! (No one would want to hear me trying to do female voices.)

Instead, I hired an incredible narrator named Heather

Masters. She's an award-winning voice actress who made my dystopian young adult thriller a riveting experience.

The bottom line is, you have options. Leverage the people around you if you don't want to do it yourself. Or reach out to my publishing agency via the link or QR code below. We're happy to help.

Igniting Souls Publishing Agency

Pave the Way for Success

People prefer your book in the format of their choice. Give them options—all the options: softcovers, hardcovers, e-books, and audiobooks.

In the coming chapters, we'll explore how to leverage your content in fourteen other streams of income.

4

INCOME STREAMS 5–7

Take a deeper dive with your content.

Are you ready to cross the threshold into book-based income streams? It's an exciting jump that will open up new worlds for you.

In this chapter, we'll look at ways you can use your content to make an even greater difference in people's lives with ongoing programs, products, and services.

#5: SELF-STUDY COURSES CREATE PASSIVE IMPACT

When people read a book, they function as spectators. They take a passive role and observe the content. It's similar to an audience *watching* a movie. They sit safely in their seats. They enjoy what they're seeing or reading, but that's as far as the interaction goes.

When you create a course based on your book, you invite attendees to experience your content. They transition from spectators to participants as they interact with your unique content. They become part of the story by taking risks and getting in on the action.

Your self-study course creates space for them to reflect and respond. It can be delivered in a variety of formats:

- A companion guidebook engages readers by asking questions and encouraging them to write out their answers.
- An online course allows participants to apply their learning as they move week-by-week through your content.
- Many courses include audio options or the ability to log in via mobile phone from anywhere in the world.

The Self-Study Income Stream allows you to enjoy passive impact and passive income. In my book *Day Job to Dream Job,* I define these terms.

Notice the difference:

- **Passive Income Business** = *Income* from a venture in which an individual does not directly participate.
- **Passive Impact Business** = *Impact* from a venture in which an individual does not directly participate.

I realized in 2010 that many readers wanted to experience my books on a deeper level. As a result, my team and I created online self-study courses for each of my books, even for my fiction book! (More on that below.)

With a self-study book-based course, clients can access the content 24/7. Best of all, you only need to create this content once, and then you can experience more influence, impact, and income for the rest of your life.

Feel free to take a peek at the websites below to see how we laid out our courses. Each one is different because each book is different. Some courses are five modules long, and others are thirty modules long.

Again, if you need any help with your own course, just reach out. We are here to help.

Your Secret Name 5 Week Journey

The Deeper Path Coaching Cohort

Dream Job Bootcamp

Elixir Project Experience/Unhackable Course

Get Help Here

Fiction Books Generate Funds, Not Just Fans

After years of hearing how the 18 Streams of Income Model would never work for fiction, I was fed up. But what could I say? I had yet to write a fiction book and test the theory.

It was 2014, and I had no plans or desire to write a fiction book, which meant the critics would simply win the debate by default. I knew in my gut the model could work perfectly for fiction. After all, fiction books are based on facts. They include relationships, conflict, and resolution. Why wouldn't they fit the model? But without a case study, my beliefs were only theoretical.

Then something changed.

On October 9, 2014, I awoke from a dream with the phrase "Elixir Project" on my lips and the idea for a fiction book brewing in my mind. The idea centered on a future society in which a sinister group hacks people's brains. The main character and her friends were born *unhackable*. They would need to leverage their superpowers to overthrow an evil organization.

After months of resisting the temptation to cross over from nonfiction to fiction, I finally summoned enough courage to start. Although *Elixir Projec*t (ElixirProject-Book.com) could be categorized as science fiction, when writing my novel, I meticulously researched many details related to flow, the optimal state of human performance.

My studies spanned the work of Mihaly Csikszentmihalyi (often referred to as the architect of *flow*) to Steven Kotler (award-winning journalist, executive director of the Flow Research Collective, and one of the world's leading experts on high performance).

The story required incredible character development, and I knew I had my work cut out for me.

I finally published the fiction book in 2016, two years after my initial dream.

The back cover copy captures the plot:

EVERYTHING CAN BE HACKED, EVEN THE TRUTH.

Will this fact set Sienna free or plunge her into an even bigger lie?

Sienna Lewis lives in a world constantly threatened by a hacktivist group known as SWARM. After SWARM executes its deadliest attack yet, Sienna and her three college friends learn they have been chosen for the ELIXIR Project —a master plan designed to overthrow SWARM—and participation is mandatory.

As she faces the deadly challenges of the Project, Sienna confronts layers of conspiracies that force her to question everyone she trusts and everything she believes about her friends, her parents' untimely deaths, and herself—all while staying one step ahead of SWARM. In this fast-paced, near-future thriller, will love and loyalty have time to catch up with Sienna? Or will she crack under the pressure of a future already chosen for her?

I launched the book at my conference based on the novel. We filled the room at $400 per seat, and I taught the 150 attendees how to become "Unhackable" in work and life. By leveraging flow, they learned how to overcome the distractions hacking their lives and businesses.

Six weeks later, I offered a thirty-day course called "Elixir Project Experience" (UnhackableBook.com/course). The course integrated my fictional story with real research derived from fields such as neuroscience, productivity, military, athletics, education, and high performance.

More than 100 people prepurchased the course priced at $500. In six weeks, this fiction book earned over six figures in sales, not counting the audiobook, e-book, paperback, and hardback sales. Three months later, we launched the *Elixir Project* Mastermind, and several dozen people joined that too.

The following months, we created and integrated many of the other income streams you'll read about in the remainder of this book. My critics stopped their negativity once I produced the income reports. (At least some of them did.)

I knew the 18 Streams of Income Model would work for fiction, and I wanted to blaze a path for fiction authors who shared my belief. I saw how the *Harry Potter* series and other fiction books created massive pop culture appeal. Although I certainly couldn't write like J.K. Rowling, I knew I could do me, and that was enough.

Almost immediately, a few of my audience members suggested that I turn the course and fiction book into a nonfiction book. Many of my readers didn't prefer fiction, and despite consuming *Elixir Project,* they also wanted a book based on hard science.

I went to work, and four years later released *Unhackable,* the nonfiction counterpart for *Elixir Project.* Here's the description for *Unhackable*:

Human knowledge once doubled every thousand years. Today, it's every twelve hours.

No wonder we can't keep up!

Welcome to the Attention Economy—where you are the product. In this digital landscape, they keep score with eyeballs and eardrums. Your attention—even for a few seconds—translates into cold, hard cash they're willing to manipulate and even hack you for.

The truth is, you're getting hacked every day, and you don't even realize it. A hack is when someone or something gains unauthorized access to a computer or a system. Want to know something scary? People can be hacked. It happens millions of times a day. Your focus is the prize—and they'll hack you to get it.

Does this sound familiar? You cleared your schedule, woke up early, and informed your family and friends you're unreachable. An entire day dedicated to finally working on your dream.

Buzz. Ring. Beep. Five minutes in, another disruption. Notifications flash across your screen. Focus. Where were you? Your phone vibrates. Now you crave a distraction and the dopamine fix. Scroll. Scroll. Who are you kidding? Productivity plummets. Morale declines. Your dream gets sidelined and sabotaged—yet again. Unless you're *Unhackable.*

Better than money, power, or connections, *Unhackable* is the new secret weapon of super achievers—the ones who live their dreams.

Kary Oberbrunner made it his mission to discover if

humans could become *Unhackable*. After a six-year exploration of neurobiology, art, science, technology, education, athletics, the military, and business, he emerged with an answer—the unmistakable elixir behind all idea achievement and productivity.

This book reveals that answer in 30 daily missions. Discover how to

Create a life you love defined by freedom, finances, and fulfillment.

Tap into your hidden ability for superhuman focus to get more done in far less time.

Organize your life around "flow"—where you feel your best and perform your best.

Wake up every day thrilled to live your dream.

Ditch the hype. Tap into hope. Science fiction has blurred into science fact. Time to become Unhackable.

Unhackable caught on and became a *Wall Street Journal* and *USA Today* bestseller. The corresponding *Unhackable* course leveraged concepts from the book and drove them deep into the hearts and minds of the attendees.

#6: LIVE COACHING LETS YOUR READERS ACCESS YOU

More access *to* you means more income *for* you. Remember, you can't serve everyone at a high level, nor should you. Bestselling leadership author Andy Stanley says, "The more successful you are as a leader, the less accessible you will become."[1]

This fact allows you to monetize live coaching as a significant income stream. Think about your favorite author. Imagine having the opportunity to be coached by him or her in a small group. Zoom and videoconferencing makes this possible. You can even record the session and send the video to clients who had to miss it.

Access to you in a live setting comes at a premium price. Of course, you can give these coaching clients access to your self-service course too. But because the course comes with your live coaching or live Q-and-A sessions, the fee for this experience can and should be offered at a much higher rate.

#7: CERTIFY COACHES TO TEACH YOUR CONTENT

One of the smartest ways for authors to increase their income is to certify other people to speak, coach, and train on their content. My team and I began this process in 2011, and today, we have hundreds of certified coaches in more than a dozen countries.

Here's how it all happened. My fourth book released in September 2010. In a matter of weeks, we realized this book was special. The book touched on an issue common to many adults and teens alike—identity.

I blended my story of overcoming self-injury with the reader's journey of discovering who God created them to be. We began receiving emails from people of various backgrounds and struggles. They told us about their newfound freedom and how they discovered a connection with their Creator, their community, and their core.

Stories of victory over suicidal thoughts, depression, prostitution, workaholism, self-harm, eating disorders, and low self-esteem poured in. I continued sharing the message as best I could, but my small team and I had reached our capacity. My day job brought its own set of challenges and commitments. And although I entertained thoughts of jumping into my dream job full-time, book sales alone didn't come close to paying the bills.

Then it happened. I received an email from Desiree Arney, a stranger in New Jersey who had been touched by the message. Long story short, after a couple of chats, I asked her to join our "team."

The word *team* was a bit presumptuous. Although we wanted to change the world, we didn't have a plan, a platform, or a paycheck. We figured passion was enough, so we kept moving forward. A few months later, we decided to have a public conference, and more than 100 people showed up.

Toward the end of the conference, we blocked off an open mic time for participants to share their thoughts about the day. The stories of transformation people shared blew us away. From the feedback at that conference, it was clear that we needed a way to multiply our impact and fund our efforts. I knew I couldn't accept every speaking gig, and although I felt a little guilty turning down some opportunities, my family and day job took precedence.

Feeling momentum, we created the Your Secret Name Team. (YourSecretName.com/ysn-team). Members of this team would be trained on and certified to share the Your Secret Name content in their coaching practices. We priced the coaching team membership at a modest fee, and in no time, we added a dozen members from all over the world, including Europe and New Zealand. Additional team members trickled in, and our influence, impact, and income increased slowly but steadily.

For more clarity as you build your own team of certified coaches, refer to the websites below. If you need help thinking through how to create your own certification program, we're only an email or QR code away.

Your Secret Name Certified Coach

Deeper Path Certified Coach

Dream Job Certified Coach

Unhackable Certified Coach

Get help here

Let Go and Watch It Grow

By now, you can probably see how each income stream builds on the previous ones. Obviously, the book comes first, but from there, you can pick and choose which income streams to create and integrate.

Some authors only add a few income streams, and other authors include all eighteen. The power of this model is that it doesn't solely depend on you. By creating a self-study course, people can interact with your content on their own time. Live coaching allows you to take a deep dive with people and develop personal relationships with them. Creating a team of certified coaches allows you to enjoy the true compounding power of your content at work.

Passive impact and passive income, terms that should sound familiar by now, expand not only your business and income success but also your ability to make a difference in the world. By putting these income streams to work for my book, I was able to ignite souls whom I'd never personally met.

I'll never forget the day that reality sank in nearly a decade ago.

One chilly Ohio afternoon, I was playing with my three children on the living room floor. I think Isabel won out with her game choice—sleeping giant. Our stomachs were full from a scrumptious Sunday lunch, and the wood in the fireplace crackled and popped. Snowflakes fell softly outside, and my wife and I smiled at each other as we tried to keep up with three active kids.

Later that evening, I checked our online coaches' group. Thrilled to read the posts, I saw that three separate team members had conducted Your Secret Name events in their own cities just that weekend. One event even took place in New Zealand.

I smiled. While I enjoyed my loved ones in the comfort of my home, our certified coaches ignited souls all over the world. They communicated this message of hope to people needing healing.

It was a win for the attendees. They were set free.

It was a win for our certified coaches. They got paid to do what they love.

It was a win for me. The book spread way beyond my control.

5

INCOME STREAMS 8–10

Your book wasn't meant to stay on the shelf.

Think of your book as a walking, talking member of your business team. Where would you like that book to go?

Correct answer? How about everywhere!

If you're starting to wrap your mind around this reality, then you are light years ahead of most authors. This is because most authors think their books are meant to sit on the shelf. You, on the other hand, know your book is meant to hit the streets, the airwaves, the internet, and the world.

In this chapter, we'll show you how to effectively employ one of the most versatile members of your team.

#8: SPEAKING PUTS YOUR BOOK ON STAGES

Earlier in my career, I spent time with John Maxwell and his ghostwriter, Charlie Wetzel. Both are incredible communicators. But both are very different types of communicators. Charlie is a writer. John is a speaker and a brilliant one at that.

If you've heard John speak, you know what I'm talking about. John was voted the Number 1 Leadership Guru in the world for many years. He was also the recipient of the prestigious Golden Gavel Award, an honor presented annually by Toastmasters International to an individual distinguished in the fields of communication and leadership.

Charlie asked me an interesting question one day. He said, "Are you a writer who speaks or a speaker who writes?"

This simple yet profound question stopped me. I asked him to explain his question. He said, "I write John's books. I'm naturally a writer. Sometimes I speak. John is the opposite. He is naturally a speaker. Sometimes he writes. Although speaking and writing are both forms of communication, people tend to lean toward one or the other."

I've never forgotten his insight or his question. By the way, my answer is that I'm a writer who speaks.

Which are you?

Your answer might be obvious or subtle. Some people love one and hate the other. Other people are decent at both. My point is not to get hung up on your preference. Instead, recognize that doing both makes you a stronger communicator.

When you speak on a topic, you master that topic in a deeper way. And when you write on a topic, you internalize it in a deeper way. *Your Secret Name* was the first book I wrote with the intention of presenting the content from stages. As I crafted that book, I intentionally incorporated illustrations, vignettes, and anecdotes within the book. I've done the same for every book I've written since.

I have a confession to make. Even though I write *knowing* that I will someday deliver the content to a live audience, still I feel awkward the first time I talk on a topic after having written a book on it. It's like putting on a new pair of shoes. I might like the way they look, but walking in them feels different from what I'm used to. Not better or worse—just different.

Initially, I want to reject the new shoes and put on my old ones because they're familiar and comfortable. For a moment, I think they might make me look stupid on stage. But then I realize growth means change, and change means leaning in to the discomfort, not running from it.

When I speak on stage, I am able to test my material and get feedback in real time. Certain word pictures connect. Others fall flat. As I work through it a few times, I find that both skills improve. By speaking on it, my writing on the topic improves. And conversely, by writing on the topic, my speaking improves.

Communicating via speaking and writing leverage different skill sets. By optimizing both, the result is often transformational for you and your audience.

So consider how or where you might speak about your book's message. And when you do get the opportunity to take your content to the stage, have fun with it. Fail. Mix it up. It's supposed to feel messy in the beginning. No one is judging you, except for you. Give yourself some grace.

Stages, especially these days, can come in the form of physical stages or virtual stages. In the past two years, despite restrictions with global travel, I've spoken on more virtual stages than ever before. Each type of stage has pros and cons. Bottom line, if you're an author, speak whenever you can. It's one of the most effective ways to sell books.

Remember, no one in the audience has your script. As an author, you step onto the stage as the expert. In the English language, we use the term "wrote the book" to prove or acknowledge expertise. I'll use it in a sentence to demonstrate.

Michael Jordan "wrote the book" on basketball.

Oprah "wrote the book" on daytime television.

Get the point?

Now fill in the blank for your own expertise.

"I wrote the book on _____."

This might be hard for you answer. Here's a little secret, though: Your audience already believes you're the expert on your book topic. It's time you start believing it yourself. The longer you ignore your genius, the more likely imposter syndrome wins out.

If something in you feels like an imposter, that's a great sign. I recently read a meme on Instagram that nailed the reason why. A colleague and influencer Alex Charfen posted:

"Imposters don't have imposter syndrome."[1]

Let that sink in.

The very fact you struggle with feeling like an imposter means you're not one. Rather, it means that you *care* about people and genuinely want to help them. So take imperfect action, starting now.

The last thing I'll say on the topic of speaking is don't undercharge for speaking—and at the same time, don't worry about making all your money through a speaker's fee. Remember, you are the published expert. Come to the stage with your content and a willingness to serve the audience. It's okay to learn as you go—and to change your fees as more opportunities arise.

Many of our authors double their fees when they release a new book.

New authors who are also new to stages may charge a speaker's fee for the first time when their book is published.

I've even spoken for free on occasion and *still* earned ten times my normal speaking fee because the organizer permitted me to offer one or more next steps from my book-based business. This is one of the many benefits of creating an integrated product suite. You have many options and multiple income streams.

In general, my advice is to charge more than you think you should and don't try making a hard sales pitch. Show up filled up and serve well. Give it all you've got, and remember to give yourself some grace.

If you need help in the area of speaking or if you need clarity on how to structure a talk that integrates your buyer's journey in a natural and effective way, then please reach out. We'd love to help set you up for success. For a sample of a speaker's website, you can view mine at:

KaryOberbrunner.com/speaking.

Speaking Page Example

#9: CONTENT MARKETING LETS YOUR AUDIENCE SAMPLE THE VALUE

Ready for an analogy?

If the 18 Streams of Income Model is the vehicle that drives your book and business to the land of success, then content marketing is the fuel that powers the vehicle.

Translation?

If you miss this section, you won't get anywhere. It's that important.

Content marketing starts with identifying the customer's needs. It attracts new customers by creating and sharing valuable free content. This type of marketing builds sustainable brand loyalty, provides valuable information to consumers, and creates future customers willing to purchase products and services.

Many times, content marketing leads back to an email

list-building strategy. Done correctly, it attracts attention, generates leads, expands your customer base, increases online sales, and strengthens brand awareness. Deeply engaged communities often form around solid content marketing.

I like it simple, so I'll break it down even further. Content marketing is *sharing your book*, rather than *sharing about your book*.

Most authors are scared to do content marketing for fear of giving away too much. We're in a weird spot. Our book is our product. Therefore, giving away our content in an interview or via social media feels strange.

Many authors worry, *if I share my book for free, then why would anyone buy it?*

This is understandable. It's how I felt with my first book. All kinds of thoughts went through my head.

How much should I share?

How much should I hold back?

If I give away all of my best stuff, then people will find out I have nothing left.

A couple of key truths helped me overcome my fears.

Truth #1: The more samples I give away the right way, the more I'll sell.

Truth #2: There's always more where that came from.

We'll unpack Truth #1 now and Truth #2 in the next section.

TRUTH #1: THE MORE SAMPLES I GIVE AWAY THE RIGHT WAY, THE MORE I'LL SELL.

Have you ever seen someone giving away free samples at the grocery store? In the United States, at Sam's Club or Costco, we have the "Jimmy Dean Sausage Person."

Here's the scenario.

You're not even hungry. You're minding your own business and shopping for groceries. You smell something amazing from a few aisles away. As you get closer, you hear the meat sizzling. The nice lady asks you, "Would you care for a free sample?"

You try a sample, and you're pleasantly surprised at how amazing it tastes.

She lets you know it's on sale today, and she hands you a coupon. When you buy two packages, you get one free. You envision cooking it at your house later that night. You thank her and put three packages in your cart.

You're happy. She's happy. Jimmy Dean is happy.

Everybody wins.

(If you're a vegetarian, the illustration breaks down at this point. And that's actually okay. Not everyone will want a sample. Just keep rolling with the illustration, and I'll drive the meaning home in a second. Or better yet, pretend it's a plant-based sausage or a favorite snack you do enjoy.)

We call this the Jimmy Dean Sausage Strategy. One of my mentors taught it to me years ago. The concept is that by giving away your product, you will sell more of your product.

Car dealerships do a form of this by getting people to come in and *test drive* the product. The Ginsu knife company tweaked the model and sold millions of knives by *demonstrating* the product.

Think about your book and author career. How do you have people do the following:

Sample your product?

Test drive your product?

Demo your product?

The good news is that with the 18 Streams of Income Model, you don't have just one product—your book. Instead, you have over a dozen other products based on your book. These different products cater to people with different needs at different price points.

This reality will open your mind to all kinds of new possibilities. Combine that reality with the fact that you have more distribution channels for your content marketing available than at any other time in human history.

Here are just a few channels where you can do content marketing based on your book. (I've included links to some of my channels to help provide some clarity.)

1. News
2. Video (youtube.com/user/KaryOberbrunner)
3. White papers
4. Infographics
5. Email newsletters
6. Case studies
7. Podcasts (IgnitingSouls.com/resources)
8. How-to guides
9. Question-and-answer articles
10. Photos
11. Blogs (IgnitingSouls.com/resources)
12. Memes or shareables
    (Instagram.com/kary.oberbrunner)
13. Vlogs (youtube.com/user/KaryOberbrunner)
14. Guest posts
15. Assessments (UnhackableBook.com/assessments)
16. Contests
17. Essays
18. Snail mail
19. Interviews

The possibilities are nearly endless. And when the right people get a taste of your content, they'll come back for more. Don't forget you can make direct income from your book-based content marketing. Vloggers and Instagram influencers leverage paid sponsors for their shows and posts. Many podcasters are now charging a fee for their show. (Google "podcast paid subscription" for examples.) And for decades authors have earned income from their book excerpts (aka: content marketing) positioned as articles in newspapers, magazines, and online.

Truth #2: There's more where that came from.

One of the major fears preventing authors from being generous with their content is the *lie* that they don't have anything else to share if they give it all away.

Lie is a strong word, and I use it intentionally. I'm committed to giving unfiltered truth to my author clients because I care about them so much. This means you too.

I was stuck for years. I had the best intentions, but I didn't know how to grow my influence, impact, and income.

I've discovered the secret isn't holding back. It's giving more. By modeling generosity rather than scarcity, we attract abundance into our lives.

Most of us have been hardwired for scarcity. It's not our fault. Rather, this scrimp-and-save mindset has been passed on from generation to generation in big and small ways. Take, for example, a simple story, meant for good.

Maybe you've heard this particular scarcity story as a child: *The early bird gets the worm.*

Usually, a well-meaning adult relayed this story to you to motivate you to action. Innocent? Seemingly. Until you unpack the proposition. Let's focus on the two main characters in this ultra-short yet influential story: the worm and the bird.

First the worm.

Notice, *the* worm?

As if there's only one worm in the entire world? The truth is that *billions* of worms populate the earth. Grab a shovel and start digging just about anywhere, and you'll find more worms than you ever wanted.

A quick Internet search reveals thousands of videos and websites devoted to starting your own worm-farming business.

The worm?

Try more than 4,400 species of worms already discovered, classified, and named by scientists!

Now, notice the *early* bird.

In our short story, why must birds compete against each other? Can't they form teams or families? Most birds live in a community and work toward a common goal.

Besides, early signifies a contest—a race. What about the punctual bird who showed up on time? Is it disqualified?

Fast-forward twenty years and examine those children who believed the early bird gets the worm scarcity story. What do you observe in people who retell that story?

You end up with adults who believe the following:

- They must compete with everyone else for limited resources.
- Fear must drive their attitudes and actions.
- Other people need to lose just so they can win.

The truth is the more I give away via content marketing, the more my business has grown. Back in 2004, I thought I'd only ever write one book. That's all I had in me at the time.

Ten books later, I'm still writing, and I have a ton more books in me. You do too. As I mentioned in the last chapter, the sooner you let go, the sooner you'll grow.

#10: LAUNCH TEAMS BUILD LOYALTY

Authors often ask me, "When should I start promoting my book?"

My answer is always, "Before you're ready."

Although I've never been pregnant, many of my author

clients have. They tell me writing a book is kind of like birthing a baby. It takes time and effort.

Whether you agree or disagree with the analogy, the point is, when do you want to tell people about your baby?

Some authors wait until the due date. They feel the pressure of their book release day coming, and suddenly, they tell the world the book is almost here. There's nothing wrong with this approach, but if you suddenly post a newborn baby pic without having mentioned the pregnancy, your online friends and far-flung family members might say, "Wow, I didn't even know you were pregnant." (Or in our example: "Wow, I didn't even know you were writing a book.")

Think about a first-time mother who is excited about her baby. She tells anyone and everyone about her joy. She facilitates gender reveal parties, baby name voting polls, baby room tours, and baby shower festivities.

The watching world feels like they're part of the process. When you bring other people along with you on the journey, via social media or in-person, you create a community.

The same is true with your book. You can invite the watching world to weigh in on naming the book and voting on the cover. (Over 1,000 people voted on the cover for this book!) You can give your family, friends, and fans a tour of the book and invite them to the book launch party.

Creating a community (UnhackableBook.com/team) around your book makes a ton of sense. Don't wait to bring them in at the end. Bring them in at the beginning. Many people will join your launch team because of you. But if you really want to create buzz, make the focus of the launch team be about the message and mission of the book, not the book itself.

By positioning your book as a solution to a problem (yes, even fiction books offer solutions to problems), you'll tap into a much bigger market.

Some authors struggle initially to make the connection between a larger issue and their content. This is because most authors are book focused rather than audience focused. Remember, back to our earlier chapters, focus on the audience you serve, not on the books you sell.

To shed some light, I'll share some examples based on my own books, so you can see how I did this.

Your Secret Name (Christian/Religion)

- 25 percent of teenage females and 10 percent of teenage males, who struggle with self-injury
- 3 percent of the population, who struggle with depression

The Deeper Path (Personal Growth/Self-Help)

- 54 percent of the population, who are not engaged at work
- 13 percent of the population, who are actively disengaged at work

Day Job to Dream Job (Business/Finance)

- 86 percent of the population, who are unhappy with their current jobs
- 34 percent of the population, who have a side hustle

Elixir Project (Sci-Fi/Thriller)

- The average teenager sends and receives 3,339 texts per month
- 58 percent of men and 47 percent of women, who suffer from nomophobia, or the fear of being without a smartphone

Unhackable (Neuroscience/Productivity)

- One in three people, who confess to checking their email in the middle of the night
- 40 percent of the population, who are addicted to their smartphones

Show Up Filled Up (Relationships/Networking)

- Authors, coaches, entrepreneurs, and speakers, who want influencers to promote them and their work
- Influencers, who are frustrated with unaware but sincere people trying to get them to partner with them

START WITH AN EVENT AND MAINTAIN MOMENTUM

I encourage authors to build their community around their book launch. Humans tend to rally around events because events drive energy. It's more difficult to sustain a movement that never ends. It's much easier to come together around an event. The benefit is that after your launch, most of the community wants to stick around, making it much easier to sustain the movement you want to create.

You can set the price of admission into your launch team a number of ways. Some authors choose free. Other authors require a preorder book proof of purchase that can be set up with a simple Google form. Still other authors like to combine a number of impact streams. They may combine the audiobook, e-book, and physical book into a bundle. We've even had some authors offer multiple levels that include many impact streams, including a course, coaching, or conference.

Although your book is a message, it also can create a movement. Don't underestimate your book or yourself. People will pay to be part of your launch team, especially if they get access to you and your book. By creating a launch team, you'll increase your influence, impact, and income.

The key is to pour on the value, overdeliver, and serve your community. Often, the more you give, the more your launch team will reciprocate appreciation in the form of word-of-mouth buzz, book reviews, and social media shares. This doesn't mean stressing out about making your party an elitist event. Your book launch party can be a simple livestream party. You don't need to create a wine-and-dine physical event.

Smart authors transition their community into a membership/subscription site after the launch. We'll dive into this income stream in the near future. For now, I'll include an example from one of my past launch teams.

If you'd like to see it in action, scan the QR code.

Sample Launch Team

Sample Book Launch Party Information

Although the launch team is absolutely free, we still require a brief application. This soft screening process ensures that we keep spammers OUT and good people—like you—IN.

Each day I give you incredible value that you can apply immediately.

1. Mission Monday

2. Tool Tuesday

3. Word Wednesday

4. Thankful Thursday

 Kary Oberbrunner with Mark LaMaster
July 31 at 9:36am

July 14 (THANKFUL THURSDAY): This week I'd love to highlight one of our VIP superstars Mark LaMaster. He's an amazing author and speaker that has a heart to help fathers train their sons to be Godly young men. He is one of our Author Academy Elite authors and an Igniting Souls Tribe member. Mark said this about joining #ElixirProject ===> "Kary has helped me transform my passion into my full-time gig! I can't wait to see what the ELIXIR Project has in store for all of us that read it!" Thanks for your presence here.

Crissy Maier, Scott Perkins and 63 others   15 Comments

Like   Comment

 Kary Oberbrunner with Tanisha Williams
July 14 at 7:50am

July 14 (THANKFUL THURSDAY): This week I'd love to highlight one of our VIP superstars Tanisha Williams. She's an amazing teacher, an author, and speaker that has a heart to help young women become all they were created to be. Tanisha said this about joining #ElixirProject ===> "Last year, one of the smartest things I ever did was to give up my trip to Hawaii, and attend Escaping Shawshank. Kary has been my AAE , DJDJ, and Mastermind coach. It would. be an honor and privilege to serve to launch this incredible book." Thanks for your presence here.

Kaye Carter, Suzanne Strawcutter Talbot and 41 others   12 Comments

Like   Comment

5. Facebook Friday

Kary Oberbrunner
July 15 at 8.33am

July 15 (FACEBOOK FRIDAY): You're all invited—live in Ohio or from anywhere in the world. We start in 3 hours. Just register here to get the details and to be sent the replay. See ya soon.
http://karyoberbrunner.com/is-fellowship I'm excited!

Jurlee Hailstone Howard, Emine Elhe and 15 others   0 Comments

Like   Comment

6. Strategic Saturday

Kary Oberbrunner
July 23 at 8.49am

July 23 (STRATEGIC SATURDAY):

Hi #ElfxirProject VIP. Ready for today's secret sauce?

In almost all non-fiction writing, STOP writing for people. Write for ONE PERSON instead. Who's that you ask? Write to your former STUCK SELF.
... See More

Suzanne Mayer Steinhart, Jon Pyfure and 43 others   28 Comments

Like   Comment

Sounds too good to be true?

The party started on July 11th, and already hundreds and hundreds of people joined the ELIXIR Project VIP Launch Experience.

Many people ask me why I'm doing this. Remember, I made a commitment to add value to our members on a daily basis for six straight months.

My goal in starting this is threefold:

1. **To serve** = Anything I do flows from a heart of service. I'm committed to add value to like-minded world changers…like you. I count it a high honor and deep privilege to serve you.

2. **To teach** = This book is one big experiment. I'm pushing boundaries and borders. I'm taking big risks in the areas of ideation, innovation, and implementation. I'm taking my 12+ year career in writing, publishing, and marketing and pushing the

limits and the edges. I'm giving you a front row seat along the way.

3. **To mobilize** = My purpose is simple: igniting souls. And my moonshot is epic: ignite one million souls by 2020. Bottom line, I can't do it alone. Throughout history whenever a tribe of people bonded together and banded together for a common purpose, the world was never the same. I created this group for Souls on Fire who are crazy enough to change the world.

Many VIP members ask me how they can help.

I'll warn you up front, our VIP members are some of the most amazing people on the planet. And once our VIP members sample the value within the group, they get excited about the book, the launch, and the content.

(*ELIXIR Project* is young adult fiction. Whether you like this genre or not is irrelevant. The principles I teach are universal and work in all genres.)

Many have asked how they can give back. I've told members about four small actions that are incredibly appreciated:

- Read the book—or sample chapters—ASAP on receipt.
- Provide feedback and engage with us via Facebook.
- Leave a review on Amazon/Barnes & Noble on launch date.
- Help spread the word about the book (we'll equip you with tools to share).

So what are you waiting for?

That's one question I can't answer. Nothing fires me up more than helping brilliant authors write, publish, and market their amazing books. Like I said, the party has already started. Now, we're just waiting on you.

Many of the people who joined my free *Elixir Project* book launch team went on to purchase the *Elixir Project* course, conference, and mastermind. Notice that I didn't make money up front, but afterward we had a wonderful payday.

For other books, I charged a fee to join the launch team up front. We priced the *Unhackable* book launch team at $50. Below I'll include the language I used to explain that opportunity. Again, scan the QR code to see how we presented the opportunity.

Sample Paid Launch Team

What if you knew how to launch your book, product, or service with a million dollars in presales? How many lives could you change?

On October 24, 2020, *Unhackable* will launch on a global stage. Our team discovered a powerful process to already do over $800,000 in sales. Our goal is $1,000,000, and we're almost there.

We're already turning this knowledge into good by helping people in need around the world. We believe we can create even more good, by showing you exactly how we did it for your future launch. Join us for this once-in-a-lifetime adventure.

What You Get
The Book: Better than money, power, or connections

—*Unhackable* is the new secret weapon of super achievers—the ones who live their dreams.

The Process: Discover our cutting-edge proven process for generating a million dollars in presales and changing a million lives.

The Community: We are a group of souls on fire committed to do good in our backyards and around the world.

The Course: The Unhackable Mini-Course. Learn how to become unhackable in work and life. Receive forever access to the Unhackable: Get Your Dream Done 5-day Mini-Course.

The Coach: Kary Oberbrunner is the CEO of Igniting Souls. He is an author, coach, and speaker who helps individuals and organizations clarify who they are, why they're here, and where they're going so they can become souls on fire, experience unhackability, and share their message with the world. In the past twenty years, he's ignited over one million people with his content.

WHAT YOU GIVE: Love, Peace, Hope. When you join the Unhackable VIP launch team or purchase copies of the Unhackable book, you change lives. We've partnered with B1G1.com to donate to over 500 causes worldwide. You'll clothe families, plant trees, dig wells, educate children, rescue women, and so much more.

WHY?

Influence: You have a story, a message, and a passion for making a difference. It's time to expand your influence.

Impact: We've partnered with B1G1.com to help people around the world in desperate need of life's most basic essentials. It's time to increase your impact.

Income: Discover how to launch your book, product, or

service with a million dollars in presales. It's time to grow your income.

Click the button below to begin the adventure of a lifetime.

It's time to prepare for your big launch.

Multiply Your Efforts

Speaking, content marketing, and launch teams all have one thing in common: they expand your reach and introduce new people to you and your book.

There's only one of you. That means your message is unique to you. It also means that if your book depends on you alone, your efforts are constrained by time, money, and energy.

But as you integrate these streams of income into your book business, you remove the constraints. You *multiply* your efforts through the power of community.

When you speak, you're delivering your content to more people at once. Each person has the potential to become a raving fan, a committed client, a certified coach, or a launch team member.

With each sample you hand out through your social media, newsletter, or podcast interview, you expand your reach and add a potential reader to your following.

And as you build a launch team of people who want to rally around your message and mission, your impact reaches into new communities.

Remember, your book isn't about you. It's about your audience. When you work *with* your audience, deliver value, and show appreciation, they introduce even more people to book, business, and brand.

6

INCOME STREAMS 11–13

> Invest in one or many—you get to choose.

The beauty of the 18 Streams of Income Model is that you only do you. This means if one of the income streams doesn't fit your style, then skip it. I have a hunch most of them will feel a little uncomfortable in the beginning. They did for me.

If you feel fear, that's normal and natural. Fear is your body and brain telling you this is new territory, that you've never been here before. This is actually a great sign. It's proof you're growing. And if you're not doing new and innovative activities, then you'll simply repeat your current results.

I know that's not what you want, or you wouldn't be reading this book. Don't run from the fear. Lean in to it.

In this chapter, we'll explore opportunities that could add a few more zeros to your bottom line while contributing to people's lives in a meaningful way.

#11: MEMBERSHIP AND SUBSCRIPTION = SMALL COST AND BIG PROFITS

In the previous chapter, I mentioned that you can transition your launch team into a membership community. If you reread that section, you'll see that I even gave you a schedule to post your content: Monday through Sunday. Many membership communities offer much less content than daily posts. I've been part of membership sites that post weekly or even monthly with a live Q-and-A session from the author.

The main strategy that makes membership communities work is developing relationships around your message.

- People come for the *cause*.
- People pay for the *content*.
- People stay for the *community*.

In your membership community, you can provide tools, checklists, ideas, and resources, such as articles, special reports, monthly newsletters, expert interviews, members-only forums, or vendor lists. You can deliver the content via hard or digital copy.

Focus your subscription service on your members. Your role is to serve, not sell. When you show your members that you genuinely care, they will continue to buy into you and your subsequent products and services.

DECIDE ON YOUR CONTENT AND THEN BATCH THE PROCESS.

Remember, your content doesn't always need to come from you. You may choose to be the regular messenger, or you may want to spotlight other members. The point is you're not alone.

As you grow your income streams, you can hire help.

Plenty of services will curate the content for you and post it according to your set schedule.

If you don't have excess money in the beginning to hire a team or a part-time assistant, then consider scholarships. When I first started, I gave a scholarship to the most engaged members. This meant they got a free subscription to the community in exchange for them serving as community leaders. We all have to start somewhere. Don't let time or money become your obstacle.

Many members will see your heart to help and jump in to offer a hand. Because the community is about the mission behind your book, people want to be part of the cause.

Most of our author clients are very busy people, just like you. As a result, they don't have time to create daily or even weekly content, so they leverage the common practice of time batching.

Also known as the Pomodoro technique, time batching is a productivity system that helps people accomplish similar tasks during a dedicated time without interruptions. Time batching minimizes distractions for more concentrated work-flow and attention to detail. It also tends to help you produce better results because you get into flow, a topic I wrote about extensively in *Unhackable*.

When you're in flow, you feel your best and perform your best. You experience lateral thinking, pattern recognition, and near-perfect decision-making. You are 500 percent more productive, and you may achieve a gamma spike similar to a eureka moment.[1]

This technique isn't hype. It's hope for authors every-where. Two of our author clients share their results:

> Without even realizing it, the past few days I've been getting in the zone. I've gotten a ton of work done with book two, the house is clean and organized, and I'm on

top of two other projects that would have normally overwhelmed me. My productivity has skyrocketed.

— NANETTE O'NEAL, AUTHOR AND
EDITOR

I've been in flow all this week, and I have accomplished so much. I can't believe it.

— TANISHA WILLIAMS, FORMER
SCHOOLTEACHER

Why is time batching so effective? Brendan Hufford, an SEO consultant, shares his experience: "Batching tasks is one of the only ways I get anything done. If I had to constantly switch between all of the seemingly infinite myriad of tasks that I work on throughout the week, I'd lose my mind. I recommend that my team batch their tasks at the same time that they time-block out their calendars."[2]

#12: HIGH-END CONSULTING—BECAUSE YOU'RE THE EXPERT

As a published author, people assume you're now an expert. You wrote the book on the subject, so don't run from the spotlight. Run to it. Success doesn't ruin you; it reveals you. And it's time to get paid for that revelation.

High-end coaching differs from the live coaching we talked about in Income Stream 6 for a few reasons, with your fee being the key differentiator. Live coaching often happens in a group, which means you can charge less to each person for the same hour of your time. When you coach people one on one, your income per hour shouldn't go down—in fact, it should go up because the client is getting your undivided attention. For years, I did half-day consulting appointments called Igniter Sessions. I found they were incredibly fulfilling for me and for my clients as well.

You may choose to consult with organizations at a premium price. This consultation could be a single event or an ongoing process. You may choose to base your consultation services on content from your book. Focus on your clients and their needs, but use your book as a framework for the personal or professional transformation they desire.

Simplify the Process

Sometimes when setting up our consultation services, we let technology, the process, and the unknowns intimidate us. We're unsure how much to charge a client, how to set up the session, and how to collect payment. We let our minds run wild.

- Should we do a free session first to demonstrate competence?
- Should we do a call or provide a videoconference link?
- Is Skype preferred?
- Should we give out our personal phone number?
- What if the session goes too long?
- Should the client prepay or pay after the session?
- What if the client doesn't pay at all?

Notice how easy it is to complicate the whole process. In the past, I let all those questions—and about a hundred more —stop me from helping people. My questions became excuses that kept me stuck.

Eventually, I created a process that removed all the confusion and ambiguity. I've been consulting on content from my books for years now. Only recently I learned about Clarity.fm.

I wish I would have tapped into this simple tool when I first started.

Clarity.fm allows authors to set up shop immediately and start consulting on topics related to their books. It literally does all the work for you. Simply create a profile, set your fee ($60 an hour minimum to $1,000 an hour maximum), and share your link. That's it.

Clients who want your expertise enter their credit card number and book a session. Clarity.fm notifies you, suggests a time, provides a neutral conference call-in number, documents the length, and charges the client appropriately.

Clarity.fm does all the prework and postwork for you and deducts a nominal fee only when you get a paying client. Here's the process in their own words:

1. Find an Expert
Browse our community of experts to find the right one for you.

2. Request a Call
At this time, you will be precharged for the estimated length of the call, based on the expert's per-minute rate.

3. Connect Directly
Call the conference line provided. After the call, the charge will be adjusted to reflect the actual length of the call.

View my Clarity.fm page at Clarity.fm/karyoberbrunner.

Sample Clarity Profile

#13: WORKSHOP IMMERSION MEANS CREATING AN EXPERIENCE

Like to travel? If so, you'll love this next income stream based around your book. I call it Workshop Immersion, and it's any off-site experience related to your book.

Fiction authors love this option because many times their stories take place in unique and interesting places.

I offer this income stream annually in, of all places, the set of *The Shawshank Redemption.*

Odd? Yes.

But here's the context for why I chose Shawshank. In *Day Job to Dream Job*, I share the staggering but unsurprising statistic that 86 percent of the population feels trapped in their day jobs. They often refer to their work experience as day-job jail. Their lack of choice, combined with the inability to escape, creates a mental prison of sorts.

With that reality in mind, I broke the book into three parts:

Part 1: *Prison*
Part 2: *Plan*
Part 3: *Payoff*

Readers start in Shawshank, their day-job *Prison*. They progress into the nine-step *Plan* to break free. The book ends with the final part, *Payoff*, where readers create their own Zihuatanejo or dream job.

People Invest in Making Memories

At the Shawshank Workshop Immersion Experience, attendees literally travel throughout the physical prison. They enter solitary confinement and spend time in a cell, journaling what the bars represent to them. Attendees write a letter to their future self, capturing the power of the moment. They evaluate the cost of remaining in captivity, and they find courage to break free.

Throughout the rest of the workshop experience, we map out a practical escape plan for them to turn their passion into a full-time gig. The content for the day is all based on my book.

To say the time in Shawshank is transformational is an understatement. We've witnessed attendees create ministries, businesses, nonprofits, books, songs, films, and movements because they took time away from the daily grind.

Most likely, none of this would have happened if we booked a hotel ballroom down the road. There's nothing wrong with a regular workshop, but the immersion experience opens people in a unique way to possibilities and truths they may never have imagined or heard in a typical conference setting.

Imagine what you could do with your own immersion experience based off of your book. The only limit is your imagination. You and your readers could travel to

- A European castle for your romance novel based in England
- The Space Center for your nonfiction book based on identifying personal moonshots
- The Rock-and-Roll Hall of Fame or Country

Music Hall of Fame for your biography on Johnny Cash

- A Colorado ski excursion for your espionage thriller

The point is that your readers connect with you and your book. They want to make memories, and when you provide an opportunity, many people will invest time and energy to do so.

Go Big, Even If You Keep It Simple

With each of these income streams, you have options. Some can be one-time events (immersion experiences), and others can be ongoing services (membership sites).

Membership sites allow you to reach many people at once with curated content. They also allow you to enlist audience members in your mission, building even stronger connections and maximizing your time.

High-end coaching and consulting can be one-on-one or one-to-many, but in either case, the value of your focused time and attention comes with a premium fee.

When you give people immersive experiences based on your book, you provide them insights they never would have otherwise encountered. This creates talk triggers and word-of-mouth advertising.

Some of these income streams require more time than others, but as you build your business and your team, you can continue to multiply your impact by delegating the right things to the right people. In doing so, you can go big, even if you keep it simple.

7

INCOME STREAMS 14–17

Internalize the message with different mediums.

By now, I hope you're starting to see how your book is only the beginning. When you invest a little time making your book consumable in different mediums, your influence, impact, and income become nearly limitless.

#14: SEMINARS AND WEBINARS SET YOU UP FOR SCALABILITY

For some readers, experiences and face-to-face communication via workshops and coaching are ideal. Other readers need a more affordable option that comes without the hassles of travel. They want your book-based content—straight from your mind and mouth—but without the experience.

Seminars and webinars offer the perfect alternative for these readers. An online seminar or webinar provides time and space for people to learn. You can make these learning opportunities as interactive as you'd like. In some groups, you may choose to assign readings, discuss learning, ask and answer questions, and even conduct debates.[1] Other seminars may be a direct delivery, with you as the presenter. The choice is up to you.

Thanks to technology, no matter how large or small your physical community is, you have access to people anywhere in the world—and they have access to you. As long as you have high-speed internet and your potential readers have an electronic device, they can purchase and access your seminar or webinar.

The beauty of this format is that if you record your seminar or webinar, you can create a passive income product that will work for you for the rest of your life. Include an interactive guidebook based on your book, and you further raise the perceived value of the webinar.

When you are creating your sales page for the webinar, create a clear title, subtitle, and list of the benefits that participants can expect. Your attendees need to know what they're buying and what problem your book-based seminar or webinar is solving. For an example, feel free to reference one of my past seminars by scanning the QR code.

Sample Seminar

#15: BOOK-BASED MASTERMINDS COMBINE MULTIPLE INCOME STREAMS

Welcome to Masterminds, one of my favorite opportunities in our 18 Streams of Income Model. I enjoy them so much because I'm able to take clients extremely deep into the book content over a period of usually one year. Because of the frequent interaction, I get to know clients personally.

Napoleon Hill defined a mastermind in his classic book *Think and Grow Rich*: "A mastermind is the coordination of knowledge and effort of two or more people, who work toward a definite purpose, in the spirit of harmony."[2]

Masterminds can range in price from free to more than $100,000 per person per year. They can be as small as a few people and as large as several dozen. They can exist exclusively online, or they can meet in exotic places around the world.

Thus far, I've integrated five of my books, all different genres (fiction and nonfiction), within my masterminds:

1. *Your Secret Name*
2. *The Deeper Path*
3. *Day Job to Dream Job*
4. *Unhackable*
5. *Elixir Project*

My longest-running mastermind is called Fire Ring. The next few pages include the information we provide to prospective participants. I want you to be able to understand the purpose and process behind it as you consider creating your own mastermind. If you find this section irrelevant to your interests or goals, feel free to skip to the next income stream. Or if you want to go even deeper, check out our Fire Ring website: FireRingMastermind.com, or scan the QR code.

Sample Mastermind

Fire Ring

The premium mastermind opportunity is for select high performers focused on increasing their influence, impact, and income.

The Preparation

Prepare your business.

Fire Ring is unlike any other experience on Planet Earth. It's a way of thinking, being, and doing. It's designed to grow you and your business exponentially.

You've invested resources and time, and as a result, you deserve a significant return on this investment. Commit to "show up filled up" during this twelve-month experience, and you will see results.

Fire Ring is all about you: your dreams and your legacy. You've created the space to make your dreams a reality, and this welcome guidebook will give you the strategies you need to leverage this experience beyond what you can ask or imagine.

Protect your workshop day.

Arrange your life and business so you can focus entirely on

the workshop. Before you come, prepare so you don't have to make any phone calls or work on any other business during your workshop. You will benefit from being present physically, emotionally, and mentally.

Taking phone calls during the workshop will steal from you and your Fire Ring members.

You'll miss valuable content and community. Personal and professional breakthroughs often occur on breaks, during mealtimes, and while chatting with your coaches and colleagues.

THE EXPECTATION

Expect Unity.

Fire Ring members protect one another and the experience by practicing guidelines:

Confidentiality. Everything discussed within Fire Ring must remain confidential. Fellow members may share sensitive situations. On our growth journey, the details along the way are sacred. To ensure a safe space for sharing, all Fire Ring members must maintain a culture of confidentiality.

Professionalism. To keep a clear focus for the workshop, please treat your fellow members as colleagues and not prospects. Please show up filled up and refrain from soliciting business.

Expect Community

Who you grow with matters. Your fellow Fire Ring members make up an amazing community. If you haven't already done so, please request to join the private Fire Ring Community group. If you ever felt alone as an entrepreneur, you can now breathe easier. You're no longer alone.

Fire Ring members often find friends, colleagues, and collaborators within this premium mastermind. Some people even consider Fire Ring their personal board of directors.

Although every member is at a different place, undergoing different circumstances, the community and coaches will bring clarity and help identify your next best step. There is no obligation; however, some Fire Ring members remain in touch outside our normal workshop times via phone, email, or video conferencing. These connection points often provide additional accountability and strategic thinking. These times are encouraged but not required.

Expect Transformation

Every detail about your workshop day is designed for maximum transformation. We've provided a brief snapshot below:

- A continental breakfast is provided for you starting at 8:00 a.m. Come join your fellow members and fuel up for an exciting day.
- The workshop starts promptly at 8:30 a.m.
- We include a ten-minute break every hour for comfort, learning, and relationship building. All day long, we provide you with tasty and healthy snacks and beverages between meals.
- A catered lunch is served at 12:00 p.m. If you have any special dietary requirements, just let us know two weeks before the workshop day, and we'll prepare accordingly.
- On the day of our workshop, Fire Ring will break for dinner at 5:30 p.m. Together we'll visit a local restaurant nearby and finish our time with stimulating conversation, personal application—and of course, scrumptious food. (Based on the unique preferences of each member, Fire Ring members will cover the

cost of their own food and beverage choices for the evening meal.)

The Implementation

Rome wasn't built in a day, and neither were you or your business. It's been said that we overestimate what we can do in one day and underestimate what we can do in one year.

We've designed Fire Ring to help create visible results. You will experience these results as you implement the path laid out before you. As promised, we will walk alongside you every step of the way.

1. Implement the Content

In Fire Ring, you will choose one of three tracks: Soul on Fire, Business, or Partner. Each track is based on unique content.

Soul on Fire Track—We use *Your Secret Name*, *The Deeper Path*, *Day Job to Dream Job*, and *Elixir Project Experience* as our core content, a different focus each quarter. In this Fire Ring, you will experience personal and professional breakthroughs. Prepare for massive gains in clarity, competence, and confidence.

Business Track—We use The Fire Path as our core content. In this Fire Ring, you will launch your product or service. Whether you're starting or scaling, you will experience business growth as you clarify your offer, strengthen your sales message, and optimize your minimum viable funnel.

Partner Track—We teach and train the Fire Ring Proprietary Partner Process© to Identify, Engage, and Establish synergistic partnerships in your industry.

2. Implement Coaching

Through the Fire Ring office hours, you will have the help you need. Leverage expert advice as your needs arise. These coaching opportunities create a depth and breadth of support tailored to your unique situation.

3. Implement Fire Ring

It's to your advantage to implement the Fire Ring. You have a unique opportunity to increase your influence, impact, and income. We've provided what you need. The stakes are high, but know this: there is no one else we'd rather pour into than *you*. We believe in you and your business.

The Framework

Who: This is a premium mastermind for select high performers, focused on increasing their influence, impact, and income.

What: This experience includes daily support, weekly accountability, monthly masterminding, and four full-day, in-person workshops. You'll have the option of choosing the track that best fits your needs: Soul On Fire, Business, or Partner. Fire Ring is uniquely designed to help educate, equip, and empower you in your next level of growth.

When: We begin on November 1 and conclude on October 31.

Where: Fire Ring includes a private online coaching community with your fellow members. We also integrate weekly accountability, monthly mastermind live video sessions, and four full-day workshops. These workshops take place in January, April, July, and October. (The October gathering occurs on the Monday immediately following the Igniting Souls Conference.) All events occur in Columbus, Ohio.

Why: Fire Ring is for those who have a message to share and an audience to serve. It brings the clarity needed both more effectively and more efficiently.

How: This year-long premium mastermind requires a one-time annual investment of $10K or 12 monthly payments of $1K for the Soul On Fire and Business Track. The Partner Track requires a one-time annual investment of $15K or 3 monthly payments of $6K.

The Details

Fire Ring is a significant investment designed to produce significant results because of four critical components:

Culture + Coaches + Community + Content = Fire Ring

Regardless of your market, target audience, or demographic, if you follow the process you will experience tangible results.

Culture—We take ownership, accountability, and responsibility for ourselves.

Coaches—Refer to the website. (FireRingMastermind.com)

Community—The community can include authors, coaches, speakers, entrepreneurs, content creators, leaders, and influencers.

Content—We use *Your Secret Name, The Deeper Path, Day Job to Dream Job*, and *Elixir Project* as our core content, a different focus each quarter. In this Fire Ring, you will experience personal and professional breakthroughs. Prepare for massive gains in clarity, competence, and confidence.

Bonus—Receive a one-on-one strategy session and lifetime certification in the Igniting Souls Team of your choice (*Your Secret Name, The Deeper Path, Dream Job Coach*, or *Unhackable* Coach).

All tracks include

- 4 Private Fire Ring 1-Day Workshops
- 4 Private Clarity Check-Ins: One-on-One 30-Minute Clarity Sessions with your Coach
- 12 Masterclasses: 12 Fire Ring Monthly Masterclasses with your Coach
- 1-Year Membership: Membership in a Private Fire Ring Community
- 52 Weeks of Coaching: Regular Weekly Office Hours with Your Coach
- 1 VIP Conference: VIP Ticket to the Igniting Souls Conference

"Sometimes the greatest rebellion is the one against your own self-limiting beliefs."

— KARY OBERBRUNNER

Use Your Book as the Text

An extra benefit of facilitating your own book-based mastermind is that your book serves as the main content to be studied. Rather than creating additional curriculum, you simply include your book as the foundational text.

Depending on how often your mastermind meets, you can break your book down into assigned reading sections. Although I offer coaching sessions throughout the month, I only conduct one monthly masterclass. It's in this masterclass where we discuss the assigned reading.

Of course, every book has a different number of chapters. Twelve divides nicely into the table of contents. With the ability to add an introduction and conclusion piece, your curriculum flow is quite flexible. I'll provide some different reading plans just to give you an idea.

10-Chapter Book
Month 1: Introduction
Month 2: Chapter 1
Month 3: Chapter 2
Month 4: Chapter 3
Month 5: Chapter 4
Month 6: Chapter 5
Month 7: Chapter 6
Month 8: Chapter 7
Month 9: Chapter 8
Month 10: Chapter 9
Month 11: Chapter 10
Month 12: Conclusion

12-Chapter Book
Month 1: Chapter 1
Month 2: Chapter 2
Month 3: Chapter 3
Month 4: Chapter 4
Month 5: Chapter 5
Month 6: Chapter 6
Month 7: Chapter 7
Month 8: Chapter 8
Month 9: Chapter 9
Month 10: Chapter 10
Month 11: Chapter 11
Month 12: Chapter 12

20-Chapter Book

Month 1: Introduction

Month 2: Chapters 1–2

Month 3: Chapters 3–4

Month 4: Chapters 5–6

Month 5: Chapters 7–8

Month 6: Chapters 9–10

Month 7: Chapters 11–12

Month 8: Chapters 13–14

Month 9: Chapters 15–16

Month 10: Chapters 17–18

Month 11: Chapters 19–20

Month 12: Conclusion

The point is there's no rigid plan. You can adapt your book and your mastermind to your preferred style and structure.

#16: CONFERENCES COULD MEAN BIG COMMITMENT WITH BIG CASH

Masterminds spread the impact created from your book over an extended time. Conferences deliver the impact in a condensed format. When you pack your content into an intense, two- to four-day period, attendees often form quick bonds with each other, you, and your book.

Getting "tired together" in large- and small-group sessions, sharing meals, and doing group activities, combined with late nights and early mornings creates a transformational experience.

At the time of the publication of this book, we've hosted our annual conference—Igniting Souls—for eleven years straight. Throughout many of these eleven years, we've built the entire conference around my latest book.

Some of these years, the conference attendees received a copy of my book in their swag bag. For more information on how we structure this multi-day event, feel free to visit the conference website: IgnitingSoulsConference.com or scan the QR code.

Sample Conference Page

You'll also find a variety of details, including pricing, different ticket packages, highlight reels, and more.

Here's a quick summary of what we're about and who we attract:

Igniting Souls Conference Is a World-Class Event for World Changers.

Each year, we gather—a select group of authors, coaches, entrepreneurs, and speakers—with a message to share and a tribe to serve. We view and do life differently because we know our identity, purpose, and direction—who we are, why we're here, and where we're going. The more clarity we gain, the more our influence, impact, and income grow.

This year, enjoy even more options. Enjoy your on-site ticket live from Columbus, Ohio, or your experiential ticket from anywhere in the world. Show up filled up and get ready for transformation in your life and business.

The most powerful weapon on earth is the human soul on fire.

#17: LEVERAGE AFFILIATES FOR NEW MARKETS

Books provide a relevant reason for like-minded professionals to spread the word about you and your business. When someone refers you to a friend or client, thanking them with an affiliate commission is an intelligent gesture. People love to spread the word about good people, products, and services. Give them an extra special thank you in the form of a check.

I hope you're thinking, "What do you mean, pay affiliates a commission? On my book?"

Nope.

Smart authors recognize their book is merely the top of the funnel. Many more income streams flow from the book. By integrating your book with these other products and services, affiliates often get more excited about sharing your book. They recognize the potential for upsells, cross-sells, and down-sells. By tracking the sale with simple affiliate-based software, everyone wins. Most CRMs (Customer Relationship Managers) include affiliate technology.

We've designed a simple affiliate-based portal for our business. You can access it here (KaryOberbrunner.com/affilates) or scan the QR code to get ideas as you design your own.

Sample Affiliate Application

I'll share one example of how I've leveraged affiliates. I linked book purchases of *Day Job to Dream Job* to the book-based course Day Job to Dream Job Bootcamp. When someone bought the book through an affiliate's link, I split the profits from course and mastermind upsells with the affiliate. As a result, it was a three-way win. The affiliates benefited with commissions. The buyers benefited with clarity. And I benefited with more influence, impact, and income. View this affiliate offer on the bonus webpage by scanning the QR code.

Sample Affiliate Opportunity

LEVERAGE A PLATFORM

Income stream 17 (Affiliates) and income stream 18 (Partnerships) are powerful because they allow authors to borrow someone else's platform. If you're not familiar with a platform, it's simply the ability to be seen and heard.

There are three ways to get a platform:

1. **Buy it:** This requires money, and it doesn't carry the weight of trust that comes with referrals.
2. **Build it:** This requires time because you're adding to your platform person by person.
3. **Borrow it:** This requires relationships. Referrals gained through affiliates and partnerships are cheaper and faster than buying or building platforms.

Borrowing platforms is both an art and a science. Many new authors complain about not having a big enough platform. They wish they had more fans and followers, rationalizing that it's difficult to sell books if no one knows who you are. It's difficult, however, for people to know who you are if they don't read your book. See the dilemma?

I understand the tension. It's how I felt for the first few years in my author career. Every author has to push through this obstacle. I finally did, and life got much easier when I discovered an eight-step proven process.

Since then, many authors have seen the results and asked for the secret. I love sharing it, and I recently wrote a book on the topic. It's called *Show Up Filled Up: How to Get What You Want Out of People and Life.* You can sample the content free by scanning this QR code.

Show Up Filled Up

Here's a little more about the book:

"You can have everything in life you want, if you will just help other people get what they want." Zig Ziglar said it. People love it. But until now, no one knew the eight steps required to actually do it.

What if you knew the hidden reason why people think what they think and do what they do? For those with noble motives, this secret can be leveraged to create wisdom and wealth, benefiting humanity for generations to come.

However, when used by people with selfish motives, this secret can be leveraged to manipulate others with the purpose of securing money, sex, and power. For reasons of potential abuses, some dismiss the secret altogether, claiming it's simply too dangerous.

Just like the gift of fire, with this secret, we can light the world or burn down a forest. Therefore, it's in everyone's best interest to use it intelligently and for creating good. That outcome is completely up to you.

In *Show Up Filled Up*, Kary Oberbrunner shares his secret to success, a proven process that helped him partner with Hollywood celebrities from *Shawshank Redemption*, share the stage with Olympic and NCAA champions, turn a young adult novel into a seven-figure empire, collaborate with global leaders in multiple industries, and help solve some of the world's biggest humanitarian challenges.

Discover how to:

- Generate what many call "luck" and "good fortune" on a daily basis.
- Establish instant credibility and influence with anyone, anywhere.
- Get everything you want out of people and life without even asking.

Learn the secret, then leverage it to create the life of your dreams.

Bottom line, don't get discouraged about the people who don't know about you or your book yet. By showing up filled up you'll be able to get noticed in a noisy world. I could share hundreds of examples of authors who found a way to borrow other people's platforms.

You'll meet some of these people in the next chapter.

INCOME STREAM 18

Enjoy endless referrals.

Fair warning: Income Stream 18 takes relationship marketing to another level. Most authors focus on *their* audience, *their* readers, and *their* clients. Very few authors focus on their *potential* partners.

When you focus, instead, on creating partnerships, you generate large clusters of clients and readers. It's the difference between focusing on an apple and an apple orchard. It's one apple versus hundreds of thousands of apples.

#18: LEVERAGE THE INFINITE PARTNERSHIP SYSTEM

I've always enjoyed partnerships because I love helping other people win. I have long valued connecting others in business and in friendships. Then I met Tyler Wagner. From our first encounter, I knew this guy was doing something different. His business didn't depend on ads for new clients, but it was exploding nonetheless.

Long story short, he shared his system for creating partnerships. I immediately saw the genius of it. We optimized the system, and now people all over the world are using it to grow their businesses without any risk or ad spend.

We call it Infinite Partnership System (IPS) (InfinitePartnershipSystem.com), and it is built around seven simple steps:

1. **Identify** the partners you can serve, not the clients you can get.
2. **Contact** the right partners. Think quality, not quantity.
3. **Schedule** in a way that makes you the buyer, not the seller.
4. **Retarget** to create relational equity.
5. **Converse** in a way that allows you to serve and not sell.
6. **Automate** with the long game in mind.
7. **Scale** to work on your business, not in your business.

Leveraging the IPS changes the way you view and do sales —forever.

Forget the days of bearing incredible risk and rolling the dice with shaky ad spend to generate sales. Take a deep breath and feel at peace again. You no longer need to forfeit control, hoping your marketing platform won't change its algorithm, block your page, or deny your ads.

IPS puts people and partnerships front and center. This proven system makes work fun again by letting you experience what got you into business in the first place.

You're about to enjoy:

Freedom—to go as you please

Finances—to earn as you wish

Fulfillment—to live as you like

IPS changed our lives and businesses. Our teams are happier and healthier, and we're having a blast creating true value in the marketplace. It's the missing piece for authors who want to break through the next level. If you want more on the system, grab the free training, and learn more, visit InfinitePartnershipSystem.com or scan the QR code:

IPS Free Training

Here are a few more reasons I love the IPS:

YOU CREATE A GAME WHERE EVERYBODY WINS.

Many times in relationships, we think there should be a winner and a loser. I disagree. I go out of my way to create a game where everybody wins. This means making sure the author wins, the publisher wins, and the marketing team wins. I work to create deals that ensure everyone involved gets what they want. I make it a point to start with the end in mind regarding marketing, partnerships, businesses, and relationships.

The contrast to this mindset, of course, is to focus on being the winner, regardless of who loses. I don't like this scenario because no one wins in the long run. Sure, you might win initially, but you also ruin your chances for long-term, mutually beneficial relationships.

Before you collaborate, ask:

What is my ultimate goal?
Who could help me reach that goal?
How can I help that person reach their goals?

Once you've clarified these answers, identify wins for all parties involved.

I'm predictable—especially when it comes to meetings. I ask the other people present, "What is the ideal outcome you want to achieve sixty minutes from now?" Then I shut up and listen.

This approach makes sense for several reasons. First and foremost, it provides a deadline. If the end time isn't agreed on, then there's no urgency. The mutually agreed-on deadline creates movement and expectations.

Their response to the question matters too. Once you know how the other person defines success, you share a common scoreboard. Before these boundaries are set, you have no idea whether you're making progress.

Defining success with others invites them to operate from the same playbook. In a real sense, it's a commitment to get on the same page.

1. You get to share your platform with them.

Every person I've met wants to be recognized for what they're good at doing. One of the ways you can honor someone and highlight *their* strengths is by sharing your platform—no matter whether it's big or small. By doing this, you offer value first.

Many times, I've brought other people onto my podcasts, live videos, and physical stages. Even when I had a small platform, I showed up filled up and honored my audience and the influencer.

Don't wait until you have a big platform to become generous. Being generous now makes your platform bigger, *faster*.

2. You get to repay your new partners with your superpower.

You have a superpower, and hopefully, you know what it is. If you're unsure, check out my Igniting Souls Trilogy: *Your Secret Name*, *The Deeper Path*, and *Day Job to Dream Job*. These books will help you get clarity around your

- **Identity**—who you are
- **Purpose**—why you are here
- **Direction**—where you are going

Once you know your superpower, use it generously to repay people for their contribution to your life.

When I invite people to speak at my conference, I often offer them my superpower rather than an honorarium for their speaking fee. Most people prefer this rather than a check. Money is easier, but it's transactional. Giving your superpower is more valuable because it's transformational.

So, what is my superpower? If you're hoping for X-ray vision or the ability to leap over a tall building, then you're going to be sorely disappointed.

My superpower is helping authors, coaches, entrepreneurs, and speakers write, publish, and market their books the right way—and turn them into eighteen streams of income.

Sometimes when our conference speakers finish and the audience gives them a standing ovation, I hop on stage and announce their book deal with our company. The audience loves it because they feel as though they have witnessed something amazing. They know something nobody else in the world knows yet. The speaker feels honored, realizing there is a huge room of people already excited about their future book. Again, it's a win-win-win.

Your superpower might not be publishing, but you do have at least one, and many people in the world need it. The more you master that superpower, the more value you can create for others. Show up filled up with that superpower, and you will be irreplaceable.

3. You get to do what you wish others would do for you.

One of my mentors recently published a book. Instead of asking my clients to buy it when it came out, I bought a copy for everyone who had registered to attend my conference—all five hundred of them.

This was my mentor's first book, and I wanted to make him feel special. I made sure he knew that his book was going to be part of an exclusive package I was sending to clients all over the world. But I didn't stop there. I asked each person who received the book to take a picture with it and post the image on all their social media channels. The posts included words of affirmation and hashtags. Everyone's love made him feel like a million bucks, and his book became a bestseller on several big lists, in part because of the buzz my clients and I helped to create.

I didn't do this to make myself look like a hero. I did this because I wished someone had done this when I first started out as an author. Nobody did, so I struggled those first few years trying to build a successful career as an author.

Leveraging the power of the Infinite Partnership System creates multiple, mutually beneficial relationships that position you and others to succeed in your unique endeavors. This will continue to grow your book, brand, and business.

INCOME STREAM 19

This one is too big not to include.

I originally put the nineteenth stream of income inside this book.

Then, my team advised me to take it out.

"It's too big," they said.

"It's too unpredictable," they warned.

I listened.

However, I knew we needed to include it as a bonus download.

With the advances in technology, it would be unwise for me *not* to include it. The truth is, I embedded the nineteenth stream of income within this book. If you're reading this via e-book, visit this link KaryOberbrunner.com/18book or scan the QR code.

Get ready to "jump down the rabbit hole."

It's deep.

The 19th Income Stream

CONCLUSION: YOUR NEXT BEST STEP

Without a business behind your book, your writing will just remain a hobby.

You picked up this book for a reason. Something inside you resonated with this message. Or maybe a friend recommended it. Or maybe you just stumbled across it by accident —except I don't believe in accidents, and my guess is neither do you.

I believe there is a greater purpose for your life—dare I say "a calling." Maybe you picked up this book because you feel called to write books. If that's true, then it also stands to reason that there are people who are *meant* to read your books.

But will they?

For years, I believed I was meant to write. So I wrote— and then wrote some more. I kept waiting for my lucky break. When it didn't come, I waited some more.

And then I blamed God.

That went on for a couple of years. I was both miserable and miserable to be around. My favorite book says, "Hope deferred makes the heart sick," and I felt plenty sick.[1]

Then, I realized that maybe while I was waiting on God, God was actually waiting on me.

Maybe the dream inside my heart to write wasn't random or misappropriated. Maybe it was my destiny, and I needed to somehow push through and bring it to fruition.

And so I did.

Look. Not everyone needs to go pro with their passion. I'll tell you from experience, however, that writing as a hobby in the margins of life, after working eight hours at my day job, with three young kids, was extremely difficult. I kept up that routine for eight years, and my mind felt the effects of the sleep deprivation.

One of the reasons I'm so passionate about the 18 Streams of Income Model is that it creates options. Rather than relying on royalties alone, you now have the freedom and ability to enjoy income flowing in multiple ways. How much, how often, and how long depends largely on you.

Start with the Basics

In this final section, I want to over-deliver by providing you with some often-overlooked basics that will help you optimize your past, present, and future books. Applying these simple tweaks will enhance your book, brand, and business.

Create Your Working Title and Subtitle.

As we near the end of this book, I want to bring us back to the beginning—all the way back to your title and subtitle.

Odd? Maybe.

But if your book title and subtitle don't connect with the intended reader, then the rest of the income streams could be a struggle to effectively implement. Whether your book is already published and you're considering republishing or your book is about to be published, examining your title and subtitle is a worthwhile exercise.

Here's a strategy I use to title nonfiction books. I call it the PINCH method, and it helps your title and subtitle reach out, PINCH your potential reader, and stop them in their tracks. (If the analogy is too much of a stretch, then just recognize that the letters in the method spell the word PINCH. We gotta have a little fun.)

P: Promise

Tim Ferriss used this component with *The 4-Hour Workweek*. His premise was so powerful it became a number one *New York Times* bestselling book. His subtitle offers three promises or benefits. In fact, he followed this pattern with his entire *4-Hour* trilogy:

- *4-Hour Workweek: Escape 9–5, Live Anywhere, and Join the New Rich*[2]
- *4-Hour Chef: The Simple Path to Cooking Like a Pro, Learning Anything, and Living the Good Life*[3]
- *4-Hour Body: An Uncommon Guide to Rapid Fat-Loss, Incredible Sex, and Becoming Superhuman*[4]

Do you see the pattern? Do you see the promises? What promises can you deliver on with your book?

I: Information

Jim Collins captured the information component with his book *Good to Great*.[5] The subtitle goes further to explain what type of information readers will receive: *Why Some Companies Make the Leap . . . and Others Don't.*

What does your book deliver to readers? Make it clear with a strong title and subtitle.

N: Need

Michael Hyatt's book *Platform* addresses a practical need for business leaders of all kinds: a strong platform, a way to be seen or heard.[6] His subtitle goes even deeper to tell us how his book will meet our needs. *Get Noticed in a Noisy World.* Then Hyatt leverages a tagline to explain the need even deeper still. *A Step-by-Step Guide for Anyone with Something to Say or Sell.*

What need does your book address? How can you work that into the text on the cover?

C: Curiosity

Mark Goodman creates curiosity with his title: *Future Crimes.*[7] His subtitle adds to the intrigue: *Everything Is Connected, Everyone Is Vulnerable, and What We Can Do about It.*

How could you craft a title that piques the interest and curiosity of potential readers?

H: Humor

Delivering Happiness by the late Tony Hsieh of Zappos Shoes, integrates humor.[8] Seth Godin admits it in his endorsement, right on the cover. "This book is so funny, true, important, and useful. Just like Tony."

How could you add or highlight humor on your book? Note, this may not be appropriate in every context, but it's worth considering. If not humor, what emotion could your cover text evoke?

Now it's your turn. Write out a couple sample titles and subtitles based on the PINCH method.

P:

I:

N:

C:

H:

For more on optimizing your book title, access the free training at MyBookHook.com or scan the QR code:

Free Author Training

Map Your Buyer's Journey

By now, you've observed that the path to producing more influence, impact, and income with your book is a journey; so is the path people take when consuming your content in its various forms. Marketers call the sales process the *buyer's journey*, and it happens in three distinct stages.

Buyers start out unaware of their problem. Eventually,

they realize their problem and explore ways to solve it. Finally, these same buyers evaluate solutions and decide which one will be best for them. These stages can be summarized as

1. **Awareness**: The buyer becomes aware they have a problem.
2. **Consideration**: The buyer defines their problem and considers options to solve it.
3. **Decision**: The buyer evaluates and decides on the right product or service provider to administer the solution.

Your book—fiction or nonfiction—can and should lead people through a buyer's journey. Patrick Lencioni, a business fable author, uses fictional stories in the beginning of his books to disarm readers. Readers often get wrapped up in the characters, but as they read, they see themselves in the story. By the time they get to the practical application portion of Lencioni's books, they consider their own businesses and behaviors and evaluate what they want to improve and how. By the end of the book, they are faced with a choice: stay stuck or experience a breakthrough.

Now it's your turn. Feel free to use the space below to think through some of these questions:

1. Awareness: How can you make your readers aware of their problem?

2. Consideration: How can you present solutions?

3. Decision: How can you lead them to a decision point?

Integrate Your Back Ads

A back ad gives your reader a next step—a way to continue the relationship. Take a look at the end of this book to see how I integrated my back ad. Notice the specific verbiage I've chosen to invite readers to connect with me in various ways. Also, scan the QR code for more examples.

Sample Back Ad

Think about your past, present, and future books. How could you integrate back ads to increase your influence, impact, and income?

Continue the Conversation with an Audio Book Intro

You can't include literal back ads in your audiobook, but you can keep the conversation going. Again, the point is to give your reader, or in this case, your listener, an invitation to take their next step with you.

I've provided a sample script for how to leverage your audiobook intro and outro as a way to lead your readers into your buyer's journey.

Sample Audiobook Intro

To experience the full benefits of this content, we encourage you to access the bonuses associated with this audiobook. Visit UnhackableBook.com/audio.

When you do, you'll discover a fantastic bonus pack that will help you on your journey to becoming *Unhackable*.

One last time, that's UnhackableBook.com/audio

And now, let's begin…

Sample Audiobook Outro

We hope you enjoyed this audiobook.

You now know how to close the gap between dreaming and doing.

As I mentioned in the beginning, to experience the full benefits of this content, we encourage you to access the bonuses associated with this audiobook. Visit UnhackableBook.com/audio

Please visit: UnhackableBook.com/audio

When you do, you'll discover a fantastic bonus pack that will help you on your journey to becoming *Unhackable*.

One last time, that's UnhackableBook.com/audio

This is a simple but effective way to invite consumers to connect with you beyond the audiobook itself.

Pick Your Launch Date

People who know me will tell you I hate two abbreviations: TBA and TBD. Can you guess why?

In terms of marketing and planning, *To Be Announced* or *To Be Determined* delivers no practical value. Instead, it simply screams ambiguity.

Clarity attracts and confusion repels. So, when you tell your audience you aren't sure when your book, product, or service will launch, you're hurting yourself. That's why part of starting with the basics is picking a launch date—and sticking to it.

When we're talking about launch dates, keep in mind that this could mean your book launch, but it might also mean your course, mastermind, or membership site launch. Regardless of the income stream, one of the first steps to making it real is picking a launch date. Putting a launch date on the calendar helps you make the mental shift from concept to commitment.

I'll pull a principle from my book *Unhackable* to drive home the point:

Humanity trades billions of messages back and forth every single day. Many of these messages go unnoticed. Add the word *urgent* and, suddenly, that same message gets special treatment. By its very definition, urgent means critical, requiring immediate action or attention.

Think about the term *urgent care*. In terms of priority, this type of facility often ranks under an emergency room but over a health care provider. What's so urgent about the word *urgent*? Or, to put it another way, why does something urgent get extra special attention?

Urgency requires action because of a baked-in deadline. If the deadline is ignored, there's a price to pay in terms of health, finances, quality, or relationships. The factor that makes something urgent is scarcity or the cost involved.

Desire without a deadline is simply a pipe dream. It's easy to be fuzzy. Writing down a date makes it real. Even if you miss the date, it creates accountability. You know whether you've made it or missed it.

Picking a deadline is important—similar to picking a destination for a road trip—without one, you're just going in circles.

To help get you moving, determine the focus and your deadline, and write down which of the income streams in this book you are going focus on first and what the launch date will be.

*My Next Stream of Income*_____

*My Launch Date*_____

Put the launch date on your calendar. Mark it down and make it real.

Get the Help You Need

As an author, you're officially one of my favorite people on the planet.

More than anything, I want you to know you're not alone. After all, writing a book can feel lonely. There's rarely an audience cheering you on. You often do battle with yourself, your excuses, and your fears.

But that's what binds us authors together. We understand each other. We know the lowest of lows and highest of highs.

Bottom line, my team and I are here for you. If you need help with anything related to your book, brand, or business, please reach out via email to support@ignitingsouls.com or using this QR code:

Get Help Here

Your message and your audience are too important not to do it the right way. We need you and your book unleashed.

Now go turn that book into eighteen streams of income.

And never forget: *Your book is NOT a business card.*

AFTERWORD: SHARE THE SECRET

I wish I would have learned these eighteen streams of income earlier in my career. If I had, I could have helped many more people and ignited many more souls.

I have one simple request as we end our journey together. If this model makes sense to you, please share this book with the people you know who need it.

Now more than ever, we need authors who turn their books into multiple streams of influence, impact, and income.

I believe in you.

—Kary

CLIENT TESTIMONIALS: THE MODEL WORKS

I'm a "words of affirmation" guy. It fills my tank when we create happy clients. Often, our authors send me a copy of their book with a handwritten card or even a personal note on the first page of the book they autograph for me. They thank our team for how we helped them turn their book into multiple streams of income.

Their kind words mean far more to me than money ever could. I save these notes and cards and reference them as a reminder of our mission to ignite souls.

Rather than including a large quantity of these testimonials in this book, I selected just a few. I want you to realize that these authors started out like all of us. At one point, they had zero followers, zero income, and zero books. They took imperfect action and their next best step, and by working with our publishing agency, they created powerful book-based businesses. I trust their words will encourage you.

"Kary has a unique capability to publish my books and get them into tens of thousands of markets across the world. He leveraged my books as lead generation tools to add millions of dollars of revenue in my company."

— DAN SULLIVAN, COFOUNDER OF STRATEGIC COACH, *WALL STREET JOURNAL* BESTSELLING AUTHOR OF *WHO NOT HOW*

"Your partnership in helping me reach new goals has been one of the most important moves in my career. I can't thank you enough other than to help in any way I can, Kary. Please let me know how we can continue to motivate others together."

— AMY SCHMITTAUER LANDINO,
BESTSELLING AUTHOR OF *VLOG LIKE A BOSS* AND INTERNATIONAL SPEAKER

"It was unreal going to my live event and seeing crowds of people buying my books and waiting in line for me to sign them and get pictures. People were crying—they were so excited to read my book. Something I dreamed about for years finally came true. Kary and his team made all this possible."

— RACHEL PEDERSEN, THE QUEEN OF SOCIAL MEDIA, AUTHOR OF *I'M THE BOSS*

"Partnering with Kary and his team was the best publishing decision I could ever make. His unique model is exactly what I needed. I sold over 50,000 books and made over one million dollars in the first year of my book launch on sales and book-based products."

— JIM EDWARDS, BESTSELLING AUTHOR OF *COPYWRITING SECRETS*, CO-FOUNDER OF FUNNEL SCRIPTS

"I hired Kary and his team to help me brand my company and help me scale different aspects of my company. My expectations were already very high, and he has exceeded them completely. He has gone well above and beyond what I would even think is necessary or is possible. I am just completely blown away by his professionalism, by his attention to detail, by the high-quality team that he surrounds himself with. I came in with one set of expectations for my company, my brand, my book, and my online course. When I first started working with him, I thought that it was just going to be a handful of things that he was going to do to help me out. I thought I was going to use one or two services. I ended up using nearly every service he offers. And he has exceeded my expectations in every single one of them. I believe that he is an incredible person to work with. He has a heart for people. He has a passion for helping people get their message out into the world, and he is as professional as they get. I believe he is the world's best in terms of writing, publishing, and marketing books.

> — JUSTIN DONALD, #1 *WALL STREET JOURNAL* AND *USA TODAY* BESTSELLING AUTHOR OF *THE LIFESTYLE INVESTOR*

BIBLIOGRAPHY

1. BOOKS AND BUSINESS CARDS ARE DIFFERENT

1. Epstein, Joseph. "Think You Have a Book in You? Think Again." *New York Times*. September 28, 2002. https://www.nytimes.com/2002/09/28/opinion/think-you-have-a-book-in-you-think-again.html.
2. Pepper, Nate. "Why Can't We Throw Away Books?" *LinkedIn*. May 2017. https://www.linkedin.com/pulse/why-cant-we-throw-away-books-nate-pepper.
3. Plaja, Luisa. "How to Write a Book Review." *BookTrust*. Accessed July 7, 2021. https://www.booktrust.org.uk/books-and-reading/tips-and-advice/writing-tips/writing-tips-for-teens/how-to-write-a-book-review.
4. Guillebeau, Chris. *The $100 Startup: Reinvent the Way You Make a Living, Do What You Love, and Create a New Future*. New York: Currency, 2012.

2. POOR AUTHORS AND SMART AUTHORS ARE DIFFERENT

1. Scott, David Meerman. *Newsjacking*. Hoboken, NJ: Wiley, 2011.

3. INCOME STREAMS 1–4

1. Keating, Lauren. "Survey Finds Most People Check Their Smartphones before Getting out of Bed in the Morning." *Tech Times*. March 2, 2017. https://www.techtimes.com/articles/199967/20170302/survey-finds-people-check-smartphones-before-getting-out-bed.htm.
2. Keating, Lauren. "Survey Finds Most People Check Their Smartphones before Getting out of Bed in the Morning." *Tech Times*. March 2, 2017. https://www.techtimes.com/articles/199967/20170302/survey-finds-people-check-smartphones-before-getting-out-bed.htm.
3. Keating, Lauren. "Survey Finds Most People Check Their Smartphones before Getting out of Bed in the Morning." *Tech Times*. March 2, 2017. https://www.techtimes.com/articles/199967/20170302/survey-finds-people-check-smartphones-before-getting-out-bed.htm.
4. Price, Rob. "1 in 3 People Check Their Smartphones in the Middle of the Night." *Insider*. September 26, 2016. https://amp.insider.com/1-in-3-people-check-smartphones-night-deloitte-study-2016-9.

5. Grothaus, Michael. "What Happened When I Gave Up My Smartphone for a Week." *Fast Company.* July 21, 2016. https://www.fastcompany.com/3061913/what-happened-when-i-gave-up-my-smartphone-for-a-week.

6. McClear, Sheila. "This Exact Percentage of People Regularly Bring Their Phones into the Bathroom." *Ladders: Fast on Your Feet.* November 21, 2019. https://www.theladders.com/career-advice/this-exact-percentage-of-people-regularly-bring-their-phones-into-the-bathroom.

7. Rodriguez, Salvador. "Most Adults Always Have Smartphone Nearby, 1 in 10 Use It during Sex." *Los Angeles Times.* July 13, 2013. https://www.latimes.com/business/technology/la-fi-tn-smartphone-nearby-1-in-10-use-during-sex-20130711-story.html.

8. Goggins, David. *Can't Hurt Me: Master Your Mind and Defy the Odds.* Muskego, WI: Lioncrest Publishing, 2018.

9. "Audiobooks Continue Their Market Rise with 16% Growth in Sales." Audio Publishers Association. Press release. https://www.audiopub.org/uploads/pdf/2020-Consumer-Survey-and-2019-Sales-Survey-Press-Release-FINAL.pdf.

10. Tracy, Brian. *Time Power.* New York: AMACOM, 2004.

4. INCOME STREAMS 5–7

1. Chmieleski, Guy. "Catalyst | Andy Stanley | Be Present." *Faith on Campus.* October 6, 2011. http://faithoncampus.com/blog/catalyst-andy-stanley-be-present.

5. INCOME STREAMS 8–10

1. Charfen, Alex. "Imposter Syndrome Meme." Instagram, July 4, 2021. Accessed July 12, 2021. https://www.instagram.com/p/CQ6Lm0WMNc3.

6. INCOME STREAMS 11–13

1. Kotler, Steven. "Flow States and Creativity." *Psychology Today.* February 25, 2014. https://www.psychologytoday.com/us/blog/the-playing-field/201402/flow-states-and-creativity.

2. Moore, Kaleigh. "How to improve productivity with time batching." *Monday Blog.* November 11, 2019. https://monday.com/blog/productivity/how-to-improve-productivity-with-time-batching/

7. INCOME STREAMS 14-17

1. Billings, Laura, and Fitzgerald, Jill. Dialogic Discussion and the Paideia Seminar. *American Educational Research Journal,* 2002;39(4):907-941.
2. Hill, Napoleon. *Think and Grow Rich.* Shippensburg, PA: Sound Wisdom, 2016.

CONCLUSION: YOUR NEXT BEST STEP

1. Proverbs 13:12 (NIV).
2. Ferriss, Timothy. *The 4-Hour Workweek: Escape 9–5, Live Anywhere, and Join the New Rich.* New York: Crown Publishers, 2007.
3. Ferriss, Timothy. *The 4-Hour Chef: The Simple Path to Cooking Like a Pro, Learning Anything, and Living the Good Life.* New York: Houghton Mifflin Harcourt, 2012.
4. Ferriss, Timothy. *The 4-Hour Body: An Uncommon Guide to Rapid Fat-loss, Incredible Sex and Becoming Superhuman.* New York: Crown Archetype, 2010.
5. Collins, Jim. *Good to Great: Why Some Companies Make the Leap...And Others Don't.* New York: HarperCollins, 2001.
6. Hyatt, Michael. *Platform: Get Noticed in a Noisy World.* Nashville, TN: Thomas Nelson, Inc., 2012.
7. Goodman, Marc. *Future Crimes: Everything Is Connected, Everyone Is Vulnerable and What We Can Do About It.* New York: Anchor Books, 2015.
8. Hsieh, Tony. *Delivering Happiness: A Path to Profits, Passion, and Purpose.* New York: Grand Central Publishing, 2010.

ABOUT THE AUTHOR

KARY OBERBRUNNER is a *Wall Street Journal* and *USA Today* bestselling author and CEO of Igniting Souls Publishing Agency. Through his writing, speaking, and coaching, Kary helps individuals and organizations to clarify who they are, why they're here, and where they're going so they can become souls on fire.

Kary struggled to find his own distinct voice and passion. As a young man, he suffered from severe stuttering, depression, and self-injury. Today, a transformed man, Kary equips people to experience *unhackability* in work and life and share their messages with the world. In the past twenty years, he has ignited more than one million people with his content. He lives in Ohio with his wife, Kelly, and their three children.

Connect at KaryOberbrunner.com

Our mission is to help authors, coaches, entrepreneurs, and speakers write, publish, and market their books the right way—and turn them into eighteen streams of income.

You have a message to share and an audience to serve.

Let us do everything else. Chat with our team today to learn how we can help.

IgnitingSouls.com/apply